# WHEN YOUR EGO THROWS A PITY PARTY – GO ALONE!

## ONE MAN'S VIEW OF LIFE, LOVE & LOSS

### FREDD CARROLL

*For my longtime friend Keri
Enjoy!*

When your Ego

# WHEN YOUR EGO THROWS A PITY PARTY – GO ALONE!

Copyright © 2023 by Fredd Carroll & Venom Studioz Media
WWW.VenomStudioz.com

ISBN: 9798865586227

All rights reserved. No part of this publication may be reproduced, distributed, or transmitted in any form or by any means, including photocopying, recording, or other electronic or mechanical methods, without the prior written permission of the publisher, except in the case of brief quotations embodied in critical reviews and certain other noncommercial uses permitted by copyright law. For permission requests, write to the publisher, addressed "Attention: Permissions Coordinator," at the address below.
VSZ_Publishing@Outlook.com
Neither the publisher nor the author shall be held liable or responsible for any loss or damage allegedly arising from any suggestion or information contained in this book.
All names and likeness have been changed to protect the privacy of actual persons and events.

Book design and marketing by Venom Studioz and Fredd Carroll
First printing edition 2023

When your Ego

# DEDICATION

Alyssa, Anthony, and Riley - you have contributed to my survival. I may be an asshole, but I am your asshole. I will always have your backs.

There are many people who have endured far worse trauma and pain. And although this isn't a competition – I am writing this book for all of us. I highly urge you to tell your story and let it educate the masses - fuck the critics – go write!

And for that woman with the whispering eye. The person who supports my life. The woman who doesn't bullshit me and always pushes me with positivity. You are a gift.

Where were you my whole life?

When your Ego

# FOREWORD

BY: Author Dana Buckmir

Trauma affects individuals in diverse ways. A friend once told me that he had recurring nightmares of fighting that disturbed his sleep. These nightmares continued for years haunting him. During the dreams he would thrash his legs and flail his arms fighting off his attacker. He never felt rested because he couldn't get a peaceful night's sleep and his fears of reliving the same nightmare kept him up, causing insomnia.

When I asked him about his childhood, he admitted that his father was physically abusive to him and his mother. He said that he was too afraid of his father to fight back. Considering that he never confronted his father, it made sense that his nightmares were an outlet to replay the violence he had experienced as an attempt to work through and resolve these conflicts.

When your Ego

The mind is powerful. The more that we refuse to confront our demons, the more they will manifest in other aspects of our lives. After my ex-boyfriend destroyed my home and threatened to kill me, I appeared remarkably put together. While living in temporary housing I continued my regular routine. I chatted up the staff, maintained relationships with my students and spent time with friends. I seemed to being doing well considering what I just survived.

A little too well. Soon after I started having panic attacks. My chest felt tight. I couldn't breathe. My thoughts raced. I felt like I was losing control of my body. The panic attacks were a symptom of unresolved trauma. My body was warning my mind that I wasn't as okay as I thought.

Like many, Fredd Carroll is no stranger to trauma. One of the recurring themes throughout his memoir, "When Your Ego Throws a Pity Party Go Alone: One Man's View of Life, Love & Loss" is trauma.

Fredd conveys his unfiltered truth in a way that is authentic and meaningful. The reader will notice, and I can attest to this knowing Fredd on a personal level that he uses humor to discuss difficult topics. Humor can be an effective tool to deal with trauma. When Fredd incorporates humor into his narrative, he's making his story more relatable.

Some topics like sexual abuse, death, addiction, and loss are too heavy for people to handle. To grow and mature we need to deep dive into those places that are dark and hidden. The ones that make us feel uncomfortable and push us to reflect. Because let's face it, life is messy. We must work through the past so we can make peace with it. What better way to do that than to share your deepest, darkest secrets with strangers?

Fredd is brave enough to go places that many people refuse to go. I applaud him for his courage and his ability to be vulnerable. It takes a skilled storyteller to compel the reader to tackle these sensitive issues and humor is an

When your Ego

effective tool. Fredd gives the reader a window into his soul with his unapologetic, sometimes brash, and witty charm that will make all of us want to confront our demons and laugh about our collective trauma.

AUTHOR DANA BUCKMIR
WWW.DanaBuckmir.com

When your Ego

# **PREFACE**

The problem with telling your story when no one knows who you are, is that no one knows who you are. Celebrity status instantly makes a trauma-based life more interesting. From a sales point of view, any recognizable name with a ghost-written memoir will typically fly from the shelves. It makes sense. I get it. I absolutely understand because I also connect more truly to fame. Who doesn't?

Let's face it, human nature is to either watch a rich and blessed well-known person crash and burn or to connect with them on their rough beginnings as they climbed the ladder of success. We all at one time or another have found joy in others' pains and triumphs, and I am not any different from most. I assume the humanizing tragedies help us every day "normal" working class persons believing in the dream.

The issue with it or the negative is that most of us are NOT of celebrity status. Most of us live a middle-class life filled with many difficulties. Some of us find happiness and others spin in circles out of control to either implode under the stress or disappear altogether. Many others simply hit rock bottom. A few of those find recovery while others only after therapeutic or medical correction can choose the option of influencing others. Each individual journey carves its own path.

Some go on to survive the remaining years without ever telling them their journey – and that's perfectly fine. There are so many ways to go, and no one issue has a clear path to an ultimate solution. In my personal journey of changing, it's fucking exhilarating to be an open book. I love being able to be honest in my faults (And there are many to choose from). Being an approval junkie is a trauma response that many of us possess. I have it – and soon you may see why.

## When your Ego

When I or you have a traumatic life, it is easily passed off as just another person who made poor decisions and caused their own dilemma. But, when it's someone recognizable, the world reacts more compassionately. We tend to treat celebrities as a sporting event and root for whatever side fills our need. And once again, I get it. It's so easy to judge someone from the comfort of our couch. It's a therapeutic mindset without any content. Just another mind fuck and a deceitful way to convince our ego's that someone is as damaged as us.

All of this makes sense in my head, but it also makes sense that the other 99 percent can be recognized and are represented. Well, meet your representative. I am a man who has unfortunately suffered things that no human should have to endure. I managed to come out clean or cleanish, on the other side. If my life was a movie scene it would most closely replicate Andy Dufrene in The Shawshank Redemption. I've crawled through miles of shit and emerged a free man on the other side.

So why can't we tell our story? Why can't we show others that everyone can suffer similarly? Why are men specifically NOT able to feel and react to being hurt without the stigma or ridicule against their manhood? Therefore, I write my stories. My life is far from being compared to others trauma, but nonetheless the trauma has happened. The way I feel and react differs from everyone else. There is no top prize for suffering. This isn't a competition and only when you share an experience, good or bad, can we evolve to assist one another.

It is time to show other men, that their problems matter. Whether it's crying, (which I rarely do.) reacting immaturely in a time of failure, or simply talking about it openly. When I was growing up through the 70's and the 80's, boys were simply told not to cry. "Be tough" – "never let them see your pain" – among many other bullshit quotes. This no longer works. The systematic failure and emergence of social media has increased both the suicide rate (specifically in men) and mental health decline among the masses. We can change that.

When your Ego

As I write this, it is August of 2022. Up to this point I have survived traumatic abuses as a child (one I will discuss openly) – A failed marriage, as well as several failed relationships. I will talk about Divorce, Religion, Suicide, Drugs and Dreams.

Nothing I mention is chronological or intended to reveal the identity of anyone involved. Chances are, if you think I am talking about you, you either feel guilty or are wrong. If it's guilt, repent. Be better today than when you caused me harm. I have so many similar transitions between different women and the same relationship failures, that there is absolutely no doubt that I play a role in their demise. My advice, if you are offended or believe my version of the assumed you is incorrect, write your own damn book.

From a positive view, I have also persevered, raised two successful children as a single parent, and managed to overcome my lack of education to become a published author. I remained steadily employed and managed somehow to never find myself on the wrong side of the law.

Overall, I made something of myself. I forged forward and with each day became a better version. Albeit not a perfect unflawed version, nonetheless, I never gave up. I have also suffered in silence. I have one child who doesn't speak to me and a grandchild I will never know. All this hurts in one form or another but learning to accept my successes and failures as temporary moments has helped, but in the end, I miss certain pieces of my family.

I am a survivor of SEXUAL ABUSE. It isn't an easy discussion, but I am NOT here to talk about the easy – I am here to talk about the hard to talk about. I have found that it does get easier the more it is openly discussed. When others can closely relate to the impact it has had on your life, it becomes a gift that could help others navigate through a similar experience more successfully. My style of active writing without a lot of fluff is certainly an acquired taste. I can apologize but I won't. My style is who I am.

When your Ego

I never took any time to heal myself when I was a younger man. I have been broken for a long, long time. But, through an unrelenting desire to be better, I worked hard and found a slow-paced way to be the best I could every day. Although I had initially chosen a path of repair by reading and doing it myself, I highly recommend professional therapy. I may have solved a few problems and become a better human but once I got myself in front of the right therapist, it opened my world up to more meaning. And there is no shame in getting help.

After getting involved as a host for a Mental Health and Addiction Recovery podcast- HAPPY HOUR with Scott H. Silverman – my whole thought process of healing changed. I began to hear the stories of survival and recovery that far exceeded my personal trauma. That is when my brain finally turned on. About 50 years too late, but nonetheless, I now had the ability to repair my past mistakes, and to learn how to deal with the prior trauma that I had little control over as a child.

It all happened while interviewing the guests who have overdosed, committed crimes, suffered assaults, clinically died, attempted suicide, and still survived. I realized that they not only survived, but they also recovered. They all had unresolved trauma as a diving board catapulting them into the deep end of the pool. After they sunk to the bottom without the ability to swim, they continually kicked and fought wildly before finding their way back to the surface.

Those are my people. They represent far more than the others. I want to hear from the fighter, the one who visited hell and fought until reemerging from its depth and beginning again. I want the person who tries. I want the person who is willing to fix themselves and that scream out "I NEED HELP."

As my friend and podcast show cohost Scott H. Silverman often says, "pressure bursts pipes"

When your Ego

let's fix our shit together. Call a friend, call a stranger – just reach out to someone.

Hopefully, this book is used to help someone out there find their solid path. I am NOT a licensed anything, I can only tell my stories and the path that made me better. If truth, honesty, vulnerability, poorly placed comedy, emotions or swearing turns you off, this book may not be for you. But if you have ever felt less or found it difficult to climb out of the hole you may have willingly or unwillingly fallen into, then let's get back to the surface together.

I want to help you relearn how to swim.

*DISCLAIMER – There will be several moments of seriousness mixed with a comical undertone. Do not read it as disrespect or as if I do not care about the issues. I am an immature clown just trying to make you smile. (An approval junkie.) I am erratic in my thoughts, and it will show in written form. Try to keep up and if any questions arise, contact me at:
VSZ_Publishing@Outlook.com

When your Ego

# **CHAPTER ONE**

## *IT BEGINS WITH AN END*

Hello, as you sleep after your long hard night, I must refrain from calling you. I enjoy your company and you so much. You make me feel safe and loved.
I am so grateful and excited for your sweet love

Me

Not too long ago, I received this text And NOT unlike most human beings capable of giving and accepting the love of another, I was elated. Two days later, she texted me that our relationship was over. I immediately called her on the phone to find out exactly what could have happened within a single day, but no direct reason was ever given. After hanging up the call, I reflected on the why and what assumptions, and they would consume me day and night.

All I could do was research past texts, emails, and phone calls. I spent many sleepless hours deciphering and putting together an answer like a heartbroken maniac. I allowed one person to control my mood, and that mood was utter despair. The struggle within- between just letting go and grasping at the emptiness, nearly reverted the old me asshole back into play.

This book began ten years ago with the thought that others could read it and would realize that they are not alone. The original

When your Ego content was a discussion of my past childhood traumas and showing the effect each one of them has had on my life. It had the stories of abuse coupled with bad decisions, which created the man who I became. But, after numerous attempts to complete it, I realized that I wasn't healing during its process. I needed to change who I have become, I needed internal work and desperate reprogramming beyond the obvious repair. Without the solution and settlement with my past, I couldn't author the book I needed to write.

    By reopening the old scars which were merely stitched closed by the longevity of time, my mental health suffered. I began to fear the past and became anxious in situations resembling the trauma that happened so many years before. The doubt flooded my mind, and the lack of energy drained me. This is when an important person in my life walked away without any warning.

Meredith Marple once said, "You cannot make someone see clarity when they've found comfort in their fog."

Sadly, this is what I was dealing with. A once vibrant and beautiful human who had chosen vanity over her own reality. She surrounded herself with friends who were living in their own misery and making sure that she too wallowed within their pains. She never recognized that when she really needed assistance, that it was me standing there – not them.

Upon our first connections, she had empathy and numerous unresolved traumas from past relationships. I fell in love with her everything but never could manage to feel the love return to me. Either I misread her love or was never enough to solve her issues. And yes, her trauma matters. I'm not a complete asshole but I am also not the cause of the initial issues that haunted her past. I was still willing to help her solve them all.

When your Ego

Although this may come off as sour grapes and a malicious retaliatory response to being dumped by her, it isn't. I knew this person when she was someone who believed in a future. I watched proudly as she rebounded from yet another failed marriage and became a better version of herself. I am unsure when she turned toward coldness, but I began seeing the changes in slow bitter self-pity moments of financial struggle, that usually somehow became about me.

Our first major breakup lasted 5 years. She began a new relationship three weeks after and I took a path of celibacy. Celibacy is a convenient excuse for an ego's definition of "I couldn't find a date to save my life." My mind became so wrapped around her new life that I gave no fair chances to anyone new who could or did enter mine. A major mistake and far too common with men.

I continued to follow her social media as she vacationed with her newfound income stream and pretended that all was well. I tail spun into unwinnable arguments with myself while watching her portray a person who I no longer knew. I'm unsure why I self-punished myself while remaining connected.

**Sidenote**: *I should mention this was NOT an instance of stalking. I merely remained "friends" online and couldn't help viewing her status's. Let's agree to call it an obsessive behavior driven by what I believed to be love and the unresolved sudden loss.*

I was and never will be a danger to anyone. It became a confusion that I teetered between both despising and loving her. I still wanted her back but was unsure if it was for the right reasons. We initially remained friendly and often communicated based around our children and their lives. At times, it felt normal. But, after viewing her new expensive trips and new friends, I just felt like her remaining connection was for pity.

When your Ego

The truth is, I just didn't want to lose. I made her problems mine, and once they resolved – she just fucking left. The hardest realization was that my own problems now had doubled. We spent so much effort working out her issues, that mine resided on the backburner. Once I sat beside my problems – I felt the metaphoric heat and the boiling had begun.

**Note to consider:** *if you are unsure why you stay and hope for another person involved with someone else to love you back, it is NOT for the right reasons. And there is no value in obsessing. That's all about your ego.*

This became a fight or die type situation. I could either work on my flaws or collapse into a fetal position and just wait to die. Dying itself is quite easy to do and unfortunately accepted. No one is coming to save you. You may get words of support, but the actions are far in between. Men specifically don't have the tools to help solve another man's issues. We are so hardwired to mind our own business that most cries for help go unheard. It's time to change the wiring and (Obviously, not all men.)

I chose to fight and put my social life aside. I got busy working on me. It wasn't fun, nor easy. The process of doing it on my own, rather than through therapy, was daunting, and a major mistake. Thinking that I had the tools to fix my issues was merely my ego and the only way to continue pretending that everything was perfectly fine. No one, even the closest people under my roof, knew that I was suffering and merely fighting just to maintain the image of fine.

My held-in and pent-up frustration often revealed itself in private. Occasionally, my children were caught in the crossfire, but I usually recognized my errors and dialed them back. My ability to make their issues a priority balanced my manic sadness for a moment. I began immersing myself uninvited into their teen lives, to their dismay. They didn't want me there, but I also didn't know how to not be there.

Now back to the woman.

## When your Ego

I never heard from this woman again. After concluding that she returned to the man that she had cheated on for me, I emailed her twice. No response. The one thing that never entered my mind was, if she were willing to cheat on one man for another, then why wouldn't she do the same to me? Of course, it is more than possible it is probable. The same man she demeaned with being less than a lover and a non-communicator.

I will never understand the mindset or coldness that a person is willing to explore. She said things that no person should ever say to another without the intention to see them through. I was merely a pawn in her game, but she masterfully executed it so well, that I find it hard to be truly angry about it. The dedication to her winning the man she truly desired outweighed any remorse for using me as the weapon.

I can appreciate a great actor in a role. I downplayed her ability to outsmart or outplay me. If her three previous marriages didn't show me her likeness to Elizabeth Taylor minus the awards, then that's on me. With a marriage license inscribed with "to whom it may concern" why did I want anything to do with her?

This is only a part of the problem. I play an equal role or sometimes more in all my failed relationships, but this specific one ended without a true reason. It wasn't my first experience with "Ghosting," but it was the most tragic. There was no resolution beyond a vague mention of me buying her a TV for Christmas. What a horrible boyfriend, A fucking TV? that if I may add, she clearly needed. Is that even a possibility? It must be more than a TV –, right?

Regardless, her silence ate me alive. That was the calculated intention. Her knowing I despise unresolved problems with unanswered questions. I find it shallow and unbecoming, but who am I to expect resolutions? Would hearing she no longer feels an attraction to me or that I sucked in bed help in any way? I doubt it. But the "ghosting" from a "Friend" festered deep until

## When your Ego

I could come to my own conclusion, of which I could be mistaken. (But I'm not.)

   I would love to take a high road and say that It's a me problem. My choices in women are often not well thought through, but this specific one was supposed to be different. They aren't degenerates, and most are viewed as good humans among their peers, but behind closed doors the truth is often revealed.

   I could go deep into private secrets because we shared them with each other. I won't, mostly because I am content with being defeated. I lost the battle; I lost the war. It sucks, but in the end, I lost someone I had assumed to be a forever friend at the very least, for whom I always did my best to help when needed.

   This is merely an example of Life, Love and Loss - all three views from this book. It took me years to become the man I am today. I changed my view, changed my goals, and focused on the things I was aware I needed to fix. You can too.

When another man replaces you, it hurts. It hurts bad. Once time goes by, you begin to realize that it is only a bruised ego. No one wants to lose. And when you lose to someone you view as less, the ego comes out of its shadow and begins to reveal itself to the world.

You begin to become a shallower version of yourself. The plans of revenge and payback start to form because you want either he or she to feel just as hurt or want their new relation to fail upon knowing what you know. I wanted to message the new guy, but in the end, why? Me telling him doesn't get her back to me and why would anyone want that person back? It all sucks. But it doesn't suck compared to what he will eventually figure out on his own. Karma is real, it exists.

On my end, my immaturity never helps. The problem with appearing bulletproof is that eventually others start to believe it too. Hurting me emotionally must have seemed impossible because when she did it – she did it in a text. I wish her all the luck in the world, and I am

When your Ego

ashamed of falling for what I had thought was a future.

I also tend to keep score, just another immature action that I have yet resolved. No one is perfect and I still hate to fucking lose. I can deal with it better than I had in the past but deep inside where my demons went to die – it burns.

HER-1     ME-0

I mentioned how passing time heals, but it isn't true for everyone and in every situation. This is my personal journey to changing who I was because of childhood trauma – not because of this woman. Your journey will take you onto several different paths, and not all of them lead to resolve. Many paths lead you deeper into the shit and you mustn't be afraid of the depths. We all have the strength to better our futures. Don't quit on yourself – be better today for you.

Upon reevaluating the situation and the ultimate result, time healed my wounds, and I learned to accept the loss. It has now been years and I rarely ever think of her or how she is doing. It's a bit uncomfortable because she was someone I wanted to see succeed. I wanted to be a part of her successes and to see her smile like she used to when we first met. Our children managed to remain close, and her boys call me often when I am needed.

I don't think I managed it the best possible way, but I did do it the only way I knew at the time. Manipulative people will always exist – people with options will usually stray – and in the end, Fuckem.' Your best option for resolve would be to walk away and consider it a gift.

Some people can tell you whatever you need to hear. They manipulate you by knowing your past and using it to their advantage. Be careful who you trust with your secrets because honestly, they aren't always asking to understand. They are downloading information to use against you as a weapon.

You can NOT be friends with your ex. You may be able to and should be friendly, but you

*When your Ego*

must never trust that person again. Cheater's cheat and once they succeed, it gets easier for them to do. The story I tell you will never be the one that she tells all her friends. Be smart, be decisive. Delete the messages, the pictures, and the emails if you must but protect your mental wellbeing. Don't ever allow a break-up to ruin your life. Trust me – your life will improve once you remove a false entity dragging you down with lies.

The lesson I needed to learn was that although I loved her with everything I had, her effort never existed. It was a one-way street, and I was driving the wrong way. People need to earn their friendship in your life and she, once all her lies and manipulations have been revealed, is NOT worthy of any part of me at all.

For far too long, men have struggled with seeking help, especially, from being hurt within a relationship. We were pre-programmed that men don't cry. Men aren't supposed to feel pain. We are meant to move forward and find another relationship. The term, "plenty of fish in the sea" often is thrown around, and our stupid brains believe it.

Sit back and ponder this conclusion. Let's think about what happens when an unresolved past from a damaged man manages to find another relationship. The chances of it being successful are low because the man has NOT grown in any way. He will repeat the same mistakes, fail, then allow his ego to reemerge.

Unless the woman is equally damaged or desperate, there is no possibility of the relationship maintaining in a healthy manner. It becomes a vicious circle. A cycle of chaos. And this is partly why the dating world is a shit show.

I have learned through my "self" therapy and focus on being better. My real clinical therapy with a licensed therapist has become a new healthy addiction that more people should explore. If you don't or aren't willing to change, neither will the relationships in your future.

It took me a long time to recognize that life isn't always fair. The truth is it isn't even fair 50

When your Ego

percent of the time. Between my upbringing and my choices – including my attraction to damaged women, I have suffered and paid for it tenfold.

    I don't feel as if I am alone in this sinking shithole of a boat. I see others trying to swim while others simply drown. I'd like to think that my ability to utilize humor as a defense mechanism makes me more buoyant. But it goes much deeper, and that is what I intend to solve with this book.

    I am willing to be critical of myself in search of difficult answers with an intention to dance around the threat of litigation when discussing past relationships. I will never reveal anyone's identity and will NOT be using actual names. The only promise I can give is that what I say – no matter the guise I hide it behind, is truth. I don't need to embellish or smear any past mistakes.

    The top one (At the time) and only woman (or so I thought) is a person that I had little trouble loving. Most people who know her have nothing but good things to say. She is sweet and caring – over the top with her intense need to fit into the shoes of the more financially fortunate, but nonetheless revered by the outside world. The real problems lie behind her closed doors, but that's her story to tell if she chooses.

Overall, she was a sham. Her beauty and false positivity brightened my dim world at a vulnerable time until she slammed shut the shades in a text message. I still can't get past the fucking text. I really felt as if we were in middle school.

These are my life choices that I take responsibility for, and my intention in these stories is to show that mistakes are repairable if you are willing to change.

**CLOSING REMARKS:**

Relationships are a partnership. Only when both individuals or all individuals (if you are into that freaky stuff) can balance their pasts with yours, then you could proceed. Talking openly

When your Ego

and honestly, even when embarrassing or difficult, can increase that relationship's success.

I am no guru or genius with all the answers. I have experience with relationships involved with past trauma, and this is a lesson involving my personal and recent successes. This isn't a guideline or foolproof answer to solving your current issues. If anything, I want you to realize you are not alone.

Most of the pleasant moments will increase with you working on yourself. Go fix your shit. Stand up and face your flaws head on. I sat on the edge of my bed and asked myself the subjective questions aloud to myself. Before laying down, I asked myself, "What can you do better tomorrow than today?" – "Why did you say such and such when angry?"

I did find my next waking day eventually began to change. My questions to myself became increasingly more difficult but holding myself accountable helped greatly. Getting yourself into therapy will increase your chances of getting complete. And that's not just in relationships, that also in life itself.

I will end this with a quote that inspires me.

> "If there is no struggle, there is no progress."
> — Frederick Douglas

When your Ego

# CHAPTER TWO

## *THE YOUTUBE WORMHOLE*

*"Egotism is the anesthetic which nature gives us to deaden the pain of being a fool."*

YouTube and whatever other streaming service you use for music videos, could quickly become your best friend in a breakup, loss, or temporary issue. It's so simplistic to type exactly what you seek and receive a list to absolve all your pains. It has so much power that it can temp even the strongest hardheaded and heartbroken recipient to partake in.

DON'T FUCKING DO IT.

When your Ego

The wallowing and your inability to take any responsibilities has taken you to the next level. You are hurting, you feel broken. The answers aren't arriving as you finish off the bottle of whatever potion you have chosen. Just short of picking up your phone to call or text your lost lover, the thought of music enters your thoughts. This level is the "I'm all alone and I feel horrible for myself, and I am right."

<u>STEER THE FUCK AWAY</u>.

But you didn't listen to me – and here we are, three hours later and your new bottle of potion is quickly entering your bloodstream. The searches have evolved, and you are ultra focused on all your feelings. Your verbs are free flowing as if a drunken poet on Adderall. Once the lyrics to a sad sap song match the intensity of your deep lonesome pity, you become a search engine expert. You have now reached the level of insanity.

What began as Breakup Songs has become Rock Songs about Women who leave you for another man. Once these gems have been exhausted, you maneuver into cheating in a relationship. Now you have unlocked a 24-hour list of the most desperate heart wrenching songs strategically presented to you in order.

You have now created an algorithm.
Congratulations!

I am just as guilty. I often use YouTube to set the tone of whatever new story on which I am working. Whether it's a new book or screenplay, the music usually caters to the mood I am seeking. For these moments, it works. I find and always have found that music motivates my moods. Even the moods where my head is up my ass.

Music has a way to balance your thoughts. Usually, if just having a typical difficult day, you could easily find an upbeat song to help you forge through it. But, if you attempt to balance a difficult day with a sad block of misery, you will find yourself falling deeper into a giant pit of shit.

## When your Ego

I personally love a beautifully written sad song. Probably because I see everything as a movie. My eyes rarely tear up within the view of others, but safely secured in my lair of Venom Studioz, I always feel free to let it flow.

When a singer writes a song that keenly feels as if it was written for you, you connect. Now the moments are easily correlated within your world. A sad song with lyrics that you assume equal your emotions, becomes that much more.

I equate it to horoscopes. Which is complete bullshit intended to manipulate your ability to suffer in silence. Every single newspaper and now online has a generic set of paragraphs that when placed properly project a message that they wrote it only for you. They didn't. It's so vaguely written that each and any one person could twist it to fit their feeling.

I also don't buy into tarot cards and palm readers. I am just a perpetual skeptic, but I equate those types of people as manipulators willing to sell their souls for your misery. But I digress…

The exact same thing is being done with a song, except with a piece of music, it wasn't manipulation. You are the guilty party. The song that you feel and think fits your life so perfectly, also fits someone with the complete opposite emotions.

Confused yet?

What I am attempting to show is that music is dependent on the listener to conclude. Most songwriters are willing to allow us to interpret their work. What you see when you hear the words is most definitely not equal to the writer's mind. Let's explore a few examples.

"Angel" by Sarah McLachlan which somehow has connected forever to the images of dying animals needing new homes. It has a soothing piano accompanied by her talented voice that somehow correlated with emaciated dogs who need your cash.

Unfortunately, "Angel" is heroin.

When your Ego

*"In the arms of the angel - Fly away from here
From this dark cold hotel room
And the endlessness that you fear
You are pulled from the wreckage - Of your silent reverie - You're in the arms of the angel
May you find some comfort here."*

James Blunt wrote a hit called "You're Beautiful" and he is quoted as saying how fucked up he thinks it is as a wedding song. It is A fitting example of using a ballad like format to appease your desperate need.

If the lyrics don't show its truth – the video for it may. Long story short – it's a stalker reveling in a stranger's beauty who is with another man. He becomes so distraught by knowing he can never be with her that he removes his shoes and clothes prior to jumping off a cliff. The end – enjoy your marriage.

And just for an example and because I love the dirtiness and how misguided the world can be. BRYAN ADAMS wrote an upbeat lil' ditty entitled "Summer of '69" and few people chose to do the math between their birth year and the title. Most are aware of the number involved and have long figured out the songs meaning. But did you consider the analogy of...

"I got my first real six-string Bought it at the five and dime Played it 'til my fingers bled Was the summer of '69"

The sexual exploration of our youth will always leave a fond memory. I adore young love.

Before I end this short ranting chapter of sadness, let me list a few of my go to sad songs recently used while drafting an upcoming novel called THE D.A.R.K.

Because the time of my writing and the mood currently swimming endlessly in my fucking head some of these may NOT make sense. Nonetheless, all can swell your emotions. Some of them for the better and some make you swallow a fifth of liquor. I personally prefer to wallow in sadness, and we will discuss that

When your Ego

crazy emotional disconnect later. For now, here's a list of ten, just for an example.
MEATLOAF – Objects in the rearview mirror
A GREAT BIG WORLD – Say something
ADELE – Someone Like you
KEITH URBAN – Tonight I want to cry
JOHNNY CASH – Hurt
JUSTIN TIMBERLAKE – Mirrors
U2 – Song for someone
JAMES BLUNT – Monsters
LABRINTH – Jealous
BON IVER – Exile

So that is just a recent list of songs that hit a chord. The people closer to me considering my heavy metal and hard rock roots may find it strange to see the opposing genres. The truth is my taste in music has always been a mixed bag. I tend to use my rock/metal to set an aggressive tone but never was worried about judgement cast upon me for what I enjoy hearing.

My influences began as a child and listening to Casey Kasem and the weekly top forty. My stepmother's album collection was filled with amazing sixties early innovators, opening my ears to many opportunities.

### The Beatles

While perusing through her albums neatly nestled on the shelves of our dining room hutch, the same exact hutch we all had, I discovered Rubber Soul and Sergeant Peppers. The covers instantly grabbed my attention. At an early age I was able to hear the simplistic yet intricate structure of a song. Long before Jon Bon Jovi quoted, "Don't bore us, get to the chorus," The Beatles had already subscribed to its mantra. I continue to enjoy most songs that they created in their long history.

### David Bowie

I no longer remember the album's title, but I can never forget the inside image. A sprawled out thin blonde-haired man naked and hanging out. It was my first excursion into the world of

When your Ego

nudity, not my last. It was both part shaming and enthralling – exhilarating and unfathomable in my tiny little mind. This was my introduction to the rockstar.

**The Turtles**
This was my first time understanding the definition of what a worldwide hit was. When Happy Togethers track played, I intuitively knew it was played often on multiple radio stations. I even remembered the lyrics and at the time had no idea that one day I would date the guitar player's ex-wife.
Life has a strange way of reminding you where you began.

There are so many influential albums, too many to mention. From Engelbert Humperdinck to early Jackson Five. I listened to all her albums and quickly fell in love with the music. I began to understand its power and although I warned you about the YouTube algorithm, I say if the music moves you one way or another, it's a gift.

Go wallow away for a brief few moments and feel sorry for your losses. Go cry, go whine and complain, bitch, moan, scream out in pain. But – return to the next day and start moving forward.

No song will solve the problem, but it can solve a brief and temporary moment.

Go fucking nuts but return and fight for your happy. Don't wallow too long in the empty gallows, trapped in the pity songs and pain. Reemerge from your darkness and keep moving forward. Manifest and get yourself in order. Every day of your life – the good and the bad ones – usually brings you closer to the one who you need.

When your Ego

# CHAPTER THREE

## *I WAS JUST A YOUNG BOY*

*"The initial trauma of a young child may go underground but it will return to haunt us."*
James Garbarino

Now we can attack a more serious conversation. By now you should understand who I am, and how I choose to tell my stories. I am not some amazing writer who titillates with amazing longform verbs. I tend to be active and try to get to the point.

    The following chapter will NOT include my typical comedic response. This is an example of me growing and understanding that there is a

When your Ego

time and place for comedy. Although, my comedy usually is misplaced, I recognize the seriousness and tragedy of sexual molestation. I'm not seeking sorrow or the laugh, I am seeking to open your eyes. This isn't a story I want to tell. It's a story that I must.

The girl next door was an attractive and supposedly sweet teen who was employed as a sitter for my sister and myself. We knew the family well, and our mothers were connected as fellow nurses. The "sitter" as I will refer to her as, for obvious reasons, was a well-adjusted and typical young girl discovering her body. I was 7 years old when she discovered mine.
I had my first sexual experience that same day.

I'm unsure if I simply do not remember or have blocked the many instances. I can't elaborate or distinguish between the first act or the last. What I can tell you is how it felt then, and how it affected my adult sex life. I can let you in on its impact. An impact that unfortunately destroyed my innocence and forged into me sadness and doubt.

It took me about 35 years to first speak of what happened to me as a child. Now, I have no issue discussing it with anyone. It is the norm with sexual assaults that secrecy is phase one. As I said, my recollection is cloudy, but I assume knowing my parents wouldn't believe me played a role. Being so young and thrust into an unknown world must have added to confusion. I also knew that my parents told me she was in charge and not to disobey. And if I can be honest, and I know this could be taken out of context, it still felt pleasurable. I never once comprehended it as being wrong.

Whenever I say it was pleasurable, most people question my meaning. The only honest way to explain it is that like consensual sexual activity, erogenous zones exist. I didn't understand those sensations, nor had developed the abilities of a post pubescent male. It's difficult to wrap your head around this unless you've experienced it similarly, and I'm not describing a scenario where I was physically

When your Ego

forced or held down as an adult had his or her way with me. I am talking about my situation. And unfortunately, my situation is happening every day.

None of the above statements dismiss my "sitter" of her actions. Nothing above is an exemption of guilt. I was a young child and didn't understand that any of this was wrong or immoral. I often think people who have not been traumatized, don't or can't understand the long-term healing process that this can cause.

I understand the use of a word such as pleasurable is not the expected verb to describe a sexual assault, and I would appreciate any input from either a professional on the subject or those who may have unfortunately suffered the same. So just to be clear, I use "pleasurable" as a descriptive emotion in the moment. It may not be the same word others would choose, but in this moment, it is my word for my story.

I think it's difficult to put yourself in the same situation if it has never happened to you. But there is a reason most young boys explore their bodies and end up holding their penis in their hands. When the person is someone that you trust or have been told to trust, the sensation of touch does not magically disappear.

The real damage is done mentally. It becomes a long-term fight that you never understand until you experience sex on your own terms. Until you can measure the scenario and the growth of maturity, you cannot understand its impact.

I was between the ages of 7 to 10. You must understand that I had no sexual knowledge beyond typical kid specific information. I knew boys had a penis and girls had a vagina. I knew A Mommy and a Daddy made a baby but had no true idea exactly how. I knew I wasn't supposed to be nude in front of others and so on. At no point had anyone mentioned other grownups touching me.

Her process involved my typical nightly routine. My recollection is of being locked in the bathroom – seated on the floor against the door as she placed my hand onto her breast. She whispered softly and gently, assumingly aware

When your Ego

that my older sister may overhear us. Her mouth then moved toward mine and her tongue licked my neck area before swishing wildly in my mouth. As she coached me onto the rules and how to kiss with my tongue, her hands would wander around my crotch. It always lasted around ten minutes before directing me to bathe and to clean my privates.

Once out of the bathroom and into my pajamas, she repeatedly mentioned that this could happen more often if I was able to keep it a secret. She swore that it needed to remain between us because others would be jealous.

Each weekend we ended up in the same scenario and my level of knowledge or grooming as it is referred to today, increased. My hands were guided by hers over her lower area, and I was instructed to roam around and inside. She would breathe differently and often helped by guiding my hand where she wanted it.

Although I say I am over the trauma of this, writing it down has a haunting feeling. I recognize the process she followed and the more I describe, the more difficult it is to say. The thought of her forcing my hands to touch her and her hands in my pants had a long-term effect. The shame, although it isn't my fault – still exists.

Like I mentioned in the beginning my recollection of time is a bit muddled. Three years feels about the proper length the molestation happened. Regardless, whether it's once or one hundred times, it's something that should never be.

Once I became truly sexually active at around seventeen. I became ultra focused on the result and not the actual activity. My mind told me it was all about the finish. I had no concerns for the woman's involvement and only selfishly thought of myself.

Sex to me was just what we did. I completely weaponized my interactions and once I was sexually satisfied, I moved to the next girl. Sex had little meaning. Love or making love didn't exist. Strangely, even throughout a marriage

When your Ego

where my ex-wife cheated on me multiple times, it never bothered me like most others are bothered by infidelity. I was hurt by the deceit, the deception, and the lies. The sex with another man never entered the argument.

So, I viewed sex as just something we did. I didn't care about how many partners a woman had or her experience levels. I never allowed jealousy or competition between others to alter my gameplan. I never cheated in a true relationship, but many times they have on me. I assume my laid-back approach and non-jealous actions gave them the green light. Now I know my old ways were fraudulent and wrong.

Today I hold relationships more honestly. I expect commitment and truth. It took me a long time to admit that all the cheating and the empty sex did damage me. It harmed my mental state. I simply just hid behind a shield of fake strength and never allowed my emotions to be real. Today, I do. I will only engage in a sexual relation with a well-intended woman. My gut instincts, although flawed and sometimes wrong, guide the direction I go. Sex for the sake of sex, does not exist any longer.

It is difficult for me to be truly open with how this makes me feel. Whenever this molestation is revealed to a friend or other, the typical response is, "Well at least it was a girl." This may be the stupidest fucking reply to the situation. I understand the response but unfortunately, I have lived the experience. It isn't all right because it was a girl. I do admit that as a straight male it may be easier to discuss, but it isn't all right. In fact, it's highly fucked up that anyone thinks that sex with a child, no matter the orientation, is all right.

I often see incidents where a female teacher carries on a relationship with a much younger student. It usually follows with comments from others mentioning the teacher's appearance and how lucky that young boy is. We must accept and protect all children of all ages. No one single human is exonerated from the crime.

When your Ego

    The only advice I can give to any child who is experiencing this, or an adult who has in their past, is to speak up. For the child, trust that an adult will believe you. If it isn't a parent or someone you trust, tell a stranger. We need to believe the abuse before investigating the accused. Not every situation will be honest or proven true, but I am willing to bet on those odds.
    If you are an adult who has suffered through your past – it's NOT too late to speak. You do NOT need to suffer endlessly due to a predator in your childhood. Go and seek a therapist who is educated on how to help you through this. You deserve it and you have so much life left to live.

    Before ending this chapter. Here's an interesting story that recently happened.

    I woke up on a Tuesday sometime in the Winter of 2020. I poured my coffee and fired up my computer to view how many people pretend to like my posts. On Facebook, I saw a friend request from someone I hadn't seen or heard from in thirty plus years. It was the "Sitter" – my past and my pain.

Before accepting or denying the request, I stalked her page. Now in her late-50's, I noticed her children and immediately thought of their safety. I viewed all these beautiful family photos and all the smiles. My mind wandered to the worse case scenarios and to my own. Did I need her to know I remember? Did I need to just let it go?

Usually, I do not know how to think before speaking. In this scenario I almost replicated a mature adult man.

Before I could decide, a message from her appeared in my chat box.

*"Hey Freddie, long time no see. Your kids are beautiful, and you seem to be doing well. I sent you a friend request. "*

I pondered and instantly remembered so many moments trapped in the bathroom with my predator. I could see the muted yellow tile and the summer breeze gently blowing open the

When your Ego

curtain above the tub. Every unwanted memory flooded back.

The words "you seem to be doing well" and "Your kids are beautiful", hit me harder than most words ever have. My new job was to make sure my kids never knew about my situation and that they never had their own stories to tell.

After typing, deleting, and retyping a reply, I paused to be sure that I was saying what needs to be said to my predator. A hundred edits later I hit enter.

*"Thanks for the message – here is my response. I am doing well…considering getting molested by you took away precious normal years. I am doing fine. Thank you."*

I stared at the chat box as she did the same type and retype. It felt as if an hour had passed when it took fifteen minutes. I didn't know if what I was messaging mattered. In my experience, the guilty who managed to escape prosecution usually were rarely forthright. Her reply was shocking.

*"I apologize for my actions and have always held some guilt. Although not a good enough excuse, I was so uncomfortable with my own body and life, that my young mind pushed me into an unwise decision. I hope you can forgive me."*

I read her response over and over for the next few hours. I didn't type or retype and still wondered if I was her only victim. After a couple of hours reflecting on her words, I responded with a thought out and edited message.

*"I appreciate your willingness to NOT deny your actions. You are NOT forgiven or forgotten."*

I made a conscious decision to delete the messages. I denied her friend request and blocked the account. A few people I have told this story to have asked why I didn't make a copy or save it. The reason was because I still

When your Ego held onto the shame and didn't want it to be discovered by my children or anyone.

It has taken me several painful years to tell my story, but the reason is that right this minute another child is being groomed the same. Even the most innocent of people is capable of the most heinous acts. Open your eyes – be aware of who is around your children.

I knew that speaking out could help others or simply stop one predator from another victim. I now understand its impact on my life. It happened to me so I could save others.

This is not an easy story to tell, and I've mentioned that prior. I'm not ashamed any longer but I am still a little broken whenever I recollect it. I hate raising unneeded red flags for today's kids, but I also hate the attention that a story like this brings forward. I don't have the answers to end the potential dangers of it happening to other kids, but I do know that no one ever asked me the questions that may have discovered this abuse.

And that's no shot at my parents. It is impossible to know and ask all the correct questions. The guilt will always lie on my predator. I fail every day to ask the proper questions to my kids. Every child is different from others. What works for me, and my family will not always transcribe to yours.

**IN CLOSING:**

I am all right today. I, unfortunately, am one of the lucky ones. A large group of the addicts you mock are victims. I would never tell you drugs is the answer, but I know from experience that if anything had an ability to make me forget – then I am trying it.

I'm not saying you must change your thinking or gut instincts. Your safety is and should be a top priority. But you could be more conscious of your compassion toward everyone. You could be nicer to that homeless man who may be dealing with his trauma.

## When your Ego

We all have our demons – let's not create new ones. The power of kindness can change the path of a stranger. You possess this inside of you. It takes a little effort but the rewards received begin to multiply.

## CHAPTER FOUR

### *EARLY LIFE TO MID-LIFE*

My parents divorced in 1972. Considering that fifty percent of marriages end this way, this is NOT a large issue in my trauma - or I never assumed it to be. Since I was merely two years old, I have no recollection of my parents living under the same roof. I also know that the divorce had nothing to do with me – (so they said.) although my older sister would point out this coincidence in a joking manner.

During this time, my single and beautiful mother would have the occasional date. This is where the "SITTER" entered. We also had, if my memory serves, a woman who rented a room and maintained us as my mother worked the nightshift at Yale Hospital. I don't know where she was during these "sitter" issues, but who cares – it's the past.

The reason I mention my early life is my speech impediment. Yes, at one time in my life, this mouth that never shuts could not speak very well. My mother, years after the impediment was repaired, would often privately quote, "And you haven't shut the hell up since."

She was right. This mouth is a nuisance. I have plenty of great moments due to my talking ability but far more times it has caused me harm. I have ruined work relations, dates, relationships and even played a small role in my marriage's failure. I have been rude, ignorant, and completely out of line. I've hurt people and lost friendships that should have never been in jeopardy.

When your Ego

I've also been fucking funny. If you don't find the line and cross it – are you even trying?

Because this portion bores me to talk about and my memory doesn't serve me well, I will make this brief.

Having a speech impediment is a debilitating flaw. I could gather the correct words in my head and feel the words in my chest. I could push them through my throat and then nothing, but illegible garbage produced from my lips. It was frustrating. My sister understood me best and my trucks became fucks until twice weekly speech therapists helped me overcome my affliction.

I have never explored whether this played any long-term trauma. A speech impediment at an incredibly young age is less impactful than one remaining into your school aged years. I did get held back in first grade due to it, but I can't remember ever being bullied or teased by it.

Today, I still retain a few phonetic struggles. For instance, I tend to break each word down into syllables similarly to how I was taught in therapy. BLUE is naturally pronounced Buh-Lou and HAWAII somehow comes out as Who-Why-EEE. IRON now is I-Earn and the list goes on and on. It may be a mix within my New England accent or just the way I'm wired.

My spelling is superb if the word is spelled as it sounds, and the impediment drove me towards the written word. An exploration into it deeper is needed, but let's fix all the other currently active fuck ups prior.

**SIDENOTE:** Coincidently, my sister and both of her daughters are now educated in speech therapy and development. All three are changing lives.

Let's move in deeper.

Both of my parents remarried quickly. Each of them had another child to whom I refer as unnecessary splits of the inheritance. This isn't true. I love and enjoy each sibling in separate ways and some more than others. In the end I

When your Ego

have three sisters to which two of them are not related. Which made Christmas time a horrible holiday that I still don't enjoy to this day. It is something I am working on because my children deserve to enjoy it.

Usually, we began at either my father or my mother's home in alternating years opening gifts. If it began with my mother, I would have very few enjoyable memories of any Christmas morning. Mostly because my stepfather was a stickler for any kind of unorganized messes and would drag in a large garbage can to dispose immediately of any wrapping.

Once the morning passed and the toys were neatly restacked in a ridiculous clean militant style, we would all head off to my stepfather's mother's home. This woman was not a nice sweet old grandmother. She was a cold and crass elderly woman with absolutely no concern for any grandchildren not related to her by blood.

My younger sister would sit on her blood related grandmother's living room floor and be showered with gifts. My older sister and I would receive nothing at all. And when I say nothing – I mean nothing. I remember the jealousy of watching that new child tear into numerous fanciful colored boxes, revealing toys. We just sat in uncomfortable clothes with nothing to do but watch. As the years rolled by, my mother recognized the bitterness toward us and no longer made us go there.

    At my father's, we received minimal stuff but under less scrutiny of the mess. My father who is a religious man, has always done his best to be a parent. We have a minimal relation, but it's respected. We have different beliefs and personalities, but I never have doubted his love.

    His flaws are numerous, as are mine. He chose religion over fathering, but he truly is a deep believer in his faith. Before I reveal his impact on my life, I want to reiterate that I do believe he did the best he could with the tools he possesses. His mistakes are human and valid.

    As a twelve-year-old, my father sat us down. My older sister, who I assume to be fifteen at the time, may not remember this moment the same. My memory serves me as this:

When your Ego

"I wanted to be open and honest with my beliefs as a parent."

I am unsure of the length of this conversation, but I remember the message. What he explained was how in the scenario of a fire or any tragedy and if he had to choose between his wife or children, that he would always save his wife. The theory as I recall, and I don't know if it is his or the Mormon belief, was that his wife could produce more children.

Although I grasp his concept, I just never understood why the fuck this needed to be said to us. Believing the theory is one thing but revealing it to the kids is another level. I personally would rather just not know. It gave me the feeling that I was unprotected. I carried this unsafe feeling into my teen years and eventually acted out.

When I say acted out, I mean the typical standard young boy bullshit. I smoked, drank, swore, and rebelled. My father will often remark that my teen years were some nightmare situations. The truth is, he really wouldn't know what I was up to since although never an absentee parent, his newly created child was the prize.

My words may seem harsh or unwarranted. A tad dramatic and overblown. My father remains and always has been a great man. His flaws – like all human's flaws have both affected me positively and negatively.

This is about the time I discovered my actual sexual awakening. Girls squeezed tightly into Jordache jeans with their high hair suddenly piqued my interest. It began as a Friday night at the park which quickly moved deep back into the swamp where a subtle waft of low tide permeated the air. That's where the early magic started. Usually, a cheap wine or liquor and whatever new love interest of the week huddled beneath the light tower. We would sip and feign the alcohol's impact which gave us the ability or an excuse to make a move. It was all young and innocent. It rarely moved beyond a French kiss or light petting.

When your Ego

    Every neighborhood had at least one girl. She was the girl sent from the heavens to teach us young boys and to help us to perfect the art of intimacy. Luckily, my area provided a few options. The main girl for us lived with a grandmother who clearly may have been deaf. If she wasn't, then she was highly unaware of the numerous young horny boys piling into her basement to spend some time with her granddaughter.
    Some would say this girl was loose or a tramp, but she didn't seem to care what others thought. We, at the time, didn't have any understanding of the inner issues she must have had. All we knew was that she did possess the skills and was willing to teach us on the fly. Because of my unfortunate previous experience, I became a late-night option. Once she finished with the unsatisfying beginners, my expertise to finish was needed.
    I know it sounds and is a disgusting and gross brief interlude. I never had sex with her, so I thought that I was safe from any sexually transmittable diseases. Of course, now I

understand the danger that I put myself in. Sometimes innocence gets lost in the shuffle. We were young, dumb, and full of cum – just willing to satisfy the other.

This girl was the girl that no one admitted they spent time with. It sounds horrible as a grown and understanding man, but at the time, she was NOT the type you wanted attached to your future list. Thirteen-year-old boys have no tools or mindset geared toward their partners needs or mental wellbeing. I do believe the boys of today are much more well-adjusted and I believe it has developed through the world's better understanding of the subject.

An evening with her consisted of a knowledge of the basepaths. 1. kissing 2. The boobs 3. The gold 4. The entry.

She was my first excursion into a world I had already learned. This time it was age appropriate and on my terms. It was horrendous. The problem with my era and the non sex discussions in the household, was everything we discovered from other means. Old moldy porn mags became our bible. The scrambled porn channels provided us with the glorious sounds of lust. But the instinct is the thought that we need to thrust at two hundred miles per hour to please a female. Between the friction, the speed, and the excitement – things ended quickly and prematurely.

Sadly, that girl traveled down a dangerous path of drugs and poor decisions. Last I heard, she was clean and sober. I doubt she looks back and sees her past as something positive. The stupidity and hormones that rage between young teens is both natural and highly irresponsible. But I remember them mostly as educational and innocent. I hope in our brief interactions that we both managed to solve each other's problems – if only for a minute.

**FINAL NOTES:**

I realize that my writing styles and memories bounce radically throughout this book. I include the good ones to balance off the insanity. I also realize someone is reading this and saying, "you think you had it rough?"

I am hoping my persistence to overcome the bullshit I endured, (whether considered typical or dramatized) is read from a perspective of story. It isn't simplistic to write both honestly and interesting at the same time.

When I began this book, it was a formatted project and laid out into a plan that in the end bored the fucking shit out of me. It was just as honest but lacked any readability. I tended to draw out the active parts with long winded bullshit. It was no less than filler in a bound black cover – A true Shit Sandwich as my late and amazing friend Steve Ceslik would say.

When your Ego

# CHAPTER FIVE

## *A SHORT MARRIAGE AND A SHORTER LIFE*

*"A man doesn't know what happiness is until he's married. By then it's too late." —Frank Sinatra*

I had known at an early age that I wanted to have a family of my own. The one provided to me obviously did their best, but I thought I deserved more. None of this is from my elder mindset but from a child's view of the fairy tale. I recognize and appreciate the family I was given, most of my issues were never known until I exposed them.

## When your Ego

    I didn't have the experience or financial means, but I had the dream. It wasn't a destiny built on love but the only way to absolve my less than lackluster childhood – at least in my own head's fog. If my parents couldn't provide me with what I believed to be a wholesome childhood I could be that much better than for my own kids.

    When I first met my wife, she was just seventeen and already the mother of a 1-year-old. The truth is that I only gave her attention to make another girl jealous. The girl that I envisioned strolling through life with was currently not speaking with me for some unknown reason – (I do know why). I figured that if I give my full sexy non-muscular self to an attractive blonde, then she would run back to me, and we could live happily ever after. That girl never bit on my metaphorical bait. We never found our romance, sadly, and remain friendly to this day. (Or have things changed since writing this? Stay tuned!)

    Throughout my single life, I often did what I could to secure a date with her, but she still has zero interest. She is the one that never has left my fucking head, and it somehow has the potential to make me crazy. Unless you have had this type of girl in your life, it's difficult to understand. She was unmatched. Throughout my marriage and the numerous others that I dated, this girl was always the one that got away. I like to blame the bait. For all the things I am, her eyes just never seemed to focus on me. I suppose it just wasn't meant to be. But I never quit my dreams.

In my inability to secure my longing desire for her, I immediately attached myself to Susan. Why wouldn't I? She was an attractive and fun girl who, based on having a child, was sexually active. Her family appeared financially secure, and she had a genuine interest in me. We spent the summer drinking cheap beer and liquor at my beachside one room dive of an apartment and happy - Or at least what I envisioned happy to be.

Unfortunately, when she drank – she drank to excess. When I say excess, I mean full tilt. I never recognized it as an issue but more viewed

*When your Ego*

it as a young woman having typical teenage fun. I often describe it as being non-daily alcoholism. In other words, whenever her lips tasted alcohol, it was on. Susan would often keep drinking until blacking out. To me, it seemed to be no more than a girl enjoying her weekend. The problem never registered until the weekend became Monday through Friday. Regardless, I asked her to be my wife.

So, here's a scenario where although my mother has voiced concerns, I went ahead with a wedding. I chose the date of August tenth -A Day after my twenty first which happened to be my grandfather's birthday. According to my mother he had requested her unborn child, me, be born on his day. My mother did her best but fell a day short. So, to be married on it made the most logical sense if logic existed at all.

It was a large wedding or as I refer to it – A business meeting for my father-in-law with a wedding as a backdrop. He invited many unknown well-dressed men who gave amazing cash gifts that were received by us happily. My father-in-law engaged in banking and was a retired colonel in the US Airforce. A proud and stoic wealthy man who enjoyed his daily fifth of vodka. Is it all starting to make sense yet?

    I didn't enjoy the wedding moment as it happened in real time. I foolishly spent my 21st birthday at a local strip club and came home drunk at 3am. By 8am I was awakened by a serenading voice singing "Get me to the Church on time" – My best friend Ruik's mother Linda then presented a massive breakfast before sending us off to the church.

    All was fine. The typical pre-marriage jitters only intensified by the remarks of another friend's father, Tom Hunt, whispering in my ear outside the side entrance to the church, "Marriage is forever – forever slowly killing you."

    Big Tom always had a way to turn a moment into a joke. It loosened me up enough to get through the bullshit vows. The sit, stand, kneel process mixed up my alcohol-soaked insides, nearly causing sickness at the altar.

    Thankfully, the church service went quickly. We held hands and happily jumped into our

When your Ego

white stretch limousine. I asked the driver to make a stop at the cemetery to pay respect to my grandparents before continuing to the reception.

   Sitting with my back to the driver, my insides started to rumble again. Susan, my now wife, sipped haphazardly from a wine bottle and unaware of my current debacle.

   I faked my way through it by swallowing the pressure erupting as the car weaved and bounced. My insides remained held in. With our arrival at the banquet facility, and the car surrounded by loved ones celebrating us, the overwhelming stomach pangs began to churn. I suppose between the current event and the night before where I soaked my innards with alcohol while watching B level pole dancers played a significant role.

   I ran from the limousine, through the small sea of guests and directly into the bathroom. While disregarding my white tuxedo, I knelt on the clean but still a potential urine splash zone and vomited into the toilet. A country club member, not a part of the wedding, never lost a beat as he gently ran his hands under the faucet.

"You must be the groom – congrats!"

The man exited. I never knew if his remark was meant as, "I see you vomiting-I understand why" or simply just an assumed acknowledgement. I sat for a moment before getting back on my feet, cleaned myself up and sauntered out as if nothing happened.

The dead hot August summer sun beat down on my already cooking body. This is when I realized that a wedding is mostly fun for the guests, but a never-ending job for the bride and groom.

The complete process of pictures, poses, greetings, hugs – followed by more pictures, dances, food, and alcohol. Now it's time to kiss your mother – hurry cut the cake – break up a fight and say farewell. It's over before it begins. A colossal waste of money that is better served as a down payment on a home.

The rest of the night flew by. We went away on a horribly planned honeymoon, it sucked with

When your Ego

her being under twenty-one and we ran out of cash. We spent the trip drunk and bored. This was the beginning of a ten-year marriage built on infidelity and lies. It was only 2 weeks until we moved to our new home to begin our lives. I thought this was an answer, but once again I was mistaken.

Long story shortened – Susan began a long-term relation with our neighbor within the first month. I had no idea, as I went off to work each day, that he was spending his free time with her. He pretended to also be my friend and my dumbass grabbed that friendship with two hands. I was never aware of their relationship until after my divorce ten years later. The guy who had become my friend, revealed it to me himself. I no longer speak with him and although I appreciate his honesty, for me it arrived ten years too late.

Between the typical struggles and our inability to love one another truly, we decided to move away to Charlotte with our daughter (her child) and 4-year-old son.

Charlotte presented itself well and gave us both employment that was beyond our wildest dreams. We made friends, raised our family, and appeared to prosper being further away from our family's input. Unfortunately, Susan's drinking leveled up - she found a whole new group of bad influences and within a year another level of infidelity arose.

She had met the man in a bowling league. I quickly caught on this time but mostly because she no longer tried to hide it. Susan no longer feared me leaving and flaunted her ability to attract other men. Eventually, this tryst ended and merely became a diving board for her to be married and single at the same time.

I had no financial way to survive on my own, so I simply rolled with the misery. I couldn't talk with my mother because of her pre-marriage warning and my maturity wouldn't allow her to be correct. I truly had a feeling of standing in mud and trying to run.

When your Ego

**SIDENOTE**: *It remains the one reason I rarely tell my children if I have a hunch or negative feeling toward someone they are dating. I will relay the message through how I choose to interact with their new choice, but never outright say it will fail. I want them to always tell me every problem. I want to remain open minded and positive that their choices can be the right ones.*

Now back to my shitshow marriage.

In between my wife's cheating, we managed to have moments of fun. Of course, whenever fun with her and I happened, nine months later a new mouth to feed would arrive. This time, with Susan's father dying, we decided a move back home to Connecticut was needed.

Back in Connecticut, a new and unknown gift was being delivered to me. Riley was born and forever changed my life. She wasn't enough to keep our marriage intact and within a year we were separated and living apart.

Susan already had a new man moved into my house and eating meals with my children. I became so numb to being cheated on, that this time it didn't bother me at all. I finally moved on and looked forward to my future.

Now I am working three jobs and around the clock. I am paying for a home that she resides in with my children, and a small apartment for myself. Being only thirty-three with a ten-year failure in my rearview mirror, helped greatly with finding dates and speaking with women at the bars. I had confidence and a dream to relive my twenties.

Being that I lived in a college area, most of my pickups were in the 21 to 24 range. It was new and exciting - it was becoming an addiction.

I found myself at the bar every night. I never missed work or paying my bills, but on my child free weekends, cocaine reentered my life. I'm not going to pretend that I didn't enjoy it. I would NOT recommend it to others but on those booze-soaked weekends, cocaine was simply a companion.

When your Ego

My newfound party life only lasted a summer. Susan was spiraling and had moved beyond alcohol and introduced prescriptions to her routine. She stopped working altogether and my life changed with a simple phone call from my 12-year-old son.

"I came home from school and moms dead on the couch."

I don't remember the rest of the conversation, but I remember driving as fast as I could. When I arrived, Susan had risen from the grave. She stood using the door as support, slurring through a nonsensical and confusing dialogue. Somehow, a different version of me appeared. I was calm and caring – soft and gentle. I asked to see the kids and she refused.
My softness dulled and I pushed my way in.
The kids were locked safely in my son's room, and he was whispering for me to get them out. I hadn't entered the home in over a year, and when I did today, words alone could never describe it. The smell alone could knock you

down. A musty wetness that stuck in your nose hairs and reminded me of my grandmothers' basement. I had to navigate through a minefield of clothes and clutter.

The dishes cascaded from the over filled sink and onto the floor —a waterfall of filth and disgust that managed to match the grimy tiled floor. My kids gathered their necessities, and I asked my son to head toward my car with his little sister.

I stayed back and tried to speak with Susan. Her eyes glazed over as she swayed in the doorway. The kids exited quickly as if the bank held hostages were being released by the robbers.

"I will get you the help you need," I said.

She mumbled incoherently as I continued.

"I will stay with you the whole time. It's either the police or check yourself in."

Susan didn't speak. She stumbled up the stairs, fell a few times and briefly walked away. I watched from the bottom of the stairwell as she reemerged. The next second, I was dodging a blue bowling ball as it bounced and ricocheted

When your Ego

off the wall, nearly missing my leg and shattering the glass door. I walked away as she screamed threats of me kidnapping our kids. This included idle threats that she would use the broken shards to slice her wrists.

**SIDENOTE:**

I had grown numb to her threats of killing herself. I have since learned that all threats of self-harm are worthy of believing. They may not go through with it and then it's no harm no foul. But, if she had, the guilt itself could eat you alive. The suicide rate among us today is alarming. There are solutions. Let's focus on the support needed. Every person matters.

I went to the police, and she was taken for an evaluation in the hospital. The bowling ball was my gift – a perfect strike in a metaphorical twist. My kids never spent another evening with their mother, and I forever got to be the father I always thought I could be. Once again, with my finances better balanced, I had my chance.

As the years went by, I adapted to the life of a single parent. It was never perfect and at sometimes probably erratic, but my effort was always there. The kids slowly adjusted. Both had issues that needed time to resolve, but both did the work and became decent humans.

Although being a fulltime parent gave me an opportunity to be the man I always wanted to be, it also conveniently allowed me to ignore my own issues. I did absolutely nothing to fix myself. I worked hard and told the world that I was O.K. It was all lies hidden under comic relief and deflections. I continued to date poorly chosen women and never had a resolution to my past.

Susan continued to spiral. There's little doubt that me taking the kids was the right decision, but it clearly played a role in her life. She bounced between men and never helped or saw the kids. She eventually lost the house and was evicted from an apartment that I co-signed for

When your Ego

her. So many different things happened that even as I type I remember another.

Since we weren't officially divorced, I had to Fasttrack the paperwork and now include full custody. The smartest thing I ever did was negotiate a tax bill we mutually owned. It was ten thousand dollars and judged to be split between us. Instead, I offered her the option to change her last name back to her birth name and I took on the full tax bill.

She agreed. The fortunate future of this could have never been foreseen, but Susan ended up getting arrested numerous times (32) in the same town and her name never matched the children's. Thus, neither of them ever had to deal with any in school teasing about their mother.

While trying to end this chapter, let me describe a cliff note of some events without going into length. So many things happened throughout the remaining years.

Susan doesn't show at our daughter's dance recital. I had purchased her ticket and she had promised to be there. After the no show, I decided to comfort my daughter with ice cream. While driving back home, we passed by the local dive bar as a fist fight poured out into the street. It didn't take long to recognize it as my former stepdaughter. Turns out, Susan decided to marry the bartender that day. I don't know if my daughter saw what I saw. She never asked and I never brought it to her attention. Later that night, as the story goes. Susan thought consummating the marriage on a barstool in front of her guests was a clever idea. In her drunken state, she fell from his lap and smashed open her head on the bar room floor.

Susan arrives at the local high school for the biggest game of the year. My son, a top ranked high school cheerleader is doing what he did best. In her drunken stupor, she decides to hoot and holler through the fence like a screaming

When your Ego

siren, which gets the attention of everyone. I soon received a call at home and my son is incredibly embarrassed. I jump in my car and speed through town with the intent of getting arrested myself. I was steaming mad. My mind raced between my angry plans of action. Once again, I did the right thing. Instead of going straight, I turned and reported the incident to the police. They were already aware and once again an ambulance was on the scene. Susan had fallen on the running track and smashed her head – again!

Susan's husband Brian – the bartender has died. His demons were numerous, and his frame was large. My best guess would be at 6 feet five and three hundred pounds or more. I had very few interactions and sporadic threats of harm from him that never came to fruition. What I did notice was the true and actual love they shared. He was good to her. She loved him.
In a show of respect, my son and I decided to attend the vigil being held at the dive bar that

evening. This is an example where I did not think things through. Once we entered, all the patrons, her friends – swarmed and slithered uncomfortably around me, shooting glares and purposeful bumps my way which I recognized as threats. I ignored it as much as possible without sacrificing my safety. I quickly located Susan and gave her my condolences before navigating my escape. Prior to our exit, an unknown younger man cornered me between the ragged pool table and antiquated jukebox while threatening me with harm. He had me blocked from the door and yelled directly in my face. His spit and whiskey breath invaded my personal space. Others gathered and functioned as a wall so no one could get between us. Luckily, the man was very drunk. I was able to slip past and out the door. All while making sure my son stayed out of it and didn't need to protect me.

These are just a few examples.

Obviously, Susan had her issues. I received a call from my youngest daughter on a Monday,

When your Ego

the early evening prior to the NCAA basketball Championship game. She said her mother was not answering her phone calls and that it was not like her to not respond back. I dismissed it, assuming she relapsed or simply was asleep. None of it felt out of line with previous experiences.

   The next hour went by in five minutes. It began with a police officer visit to an old address where my son used to live. That current tenant contacted him at his new home in Utah, and then he reached out to me to explain the situation.

   It all ended quickly when my daughter decided to drive over to her house. Sadly, I tried to talk her out of it. I wrongly thought Susan had manipulated the situation and attempted a scam with my son's social security. This thinking also wasn't out of thin air and in hindsight was perfectly rational thinking on my part. I just needed my daughter to enjoy her night. Her whole life was spent as the parent to her own mother, and she had plans to watch the basketball game with her friends.

Upon my daughter's arrival at her mother's, the police presence gave her the message she had regrettably already known. She trusted her gut to check up on her mother and the result - unfortunate.

Susan was gone.

I arrived within three minutes and quickly did everything I could to get my child away from the scene. She agreed and left before I had gathered information from the police, and I entered the home.

The voices spoke softly. No one was in a hurry to save her, and the air had a different feeling. When I entered her room, she just lay there peacefully with her hands by her side. A few uncapped pill bottles on a bedside table caught my attention and everything else simply blurred. I was seeing her through a lens as if on a film set. None of it felt real.

I didn't react poorly and in that moment I matured. I understood my life was changing whether I wanted it to or not. She wasn't my

When your Ego

friend nor my wife any longer. We had no relation beyond our children, but that alone was enough. I felt like a failure for some unknown reason. I hurt and I didn't know why until I sat back and allowed the hurt to occur.

What I realized that day was that I allowed bitterness and my ego to get in the way of helping a human being. I knew of her daily struggles, and because I wasn't getting the money from her to support our children, I chose to ignore her cries for help.

Regardless of our failures and rocky relation, we did at one time choose to marry. The marriage failed but the children it created deserved a healthy mother. I am not saying she shouldn't have taken responsibility for her actions, but I am saying that some people just can't do it on their own.

I hold myself accountable for not being the better person, the man I know I can be or should have been. Susan obviously didn't help herself in many ways, but she wasn't discardable or a throwaway. She was a decent human who took the wrong path. Her mental health and chemical imbalances had been misdiagnosed, ignored by her, and grew into a tragic ending. I know, and her children know that she loved them the best she knew how.

The tragedy I now realize is not helping when we can or should. I personally enjoy the change in my thinking that her death created. I make sure to see the signs and I choose to reach out. Seeing my daughter push through her loss and take charge to fund her mother's burial has made me proud tremendously. She did the respected and adult things that a young woman should never have to worry about.

If you have never dealt with the cost and the planning of a burial, you'd be shocked at the impact on your grieving process. They have many options. Due to Susan's lack of planning, the cost fell upon my children and myself. Riley quickly took charge.

In the end, we provided Susan with a deserving goodbye. The kids chose to cremate and have a beachside gathering to memorialize her. I won't say it was perfect, but it was respectful.

Susan is gone but, in this home, she won't be forgotten. We forgive her issues and the way she lived, and we understand better now that addiction played a larger role.

**FINAL NOTES:**

It is so easy to be the asshole in a divorce. That's not a good enough excuse compared to how easy it is to not be one. Our children didn't ask for this life – we provided it. The least we could have done was to try and be better parents.

Susan and I never found a common ground. Our marriage was a harsh lesson in misery and struggle. We both are to blame. Life isn't perfect and being a parent isn't easy. It truly takes two to produce the best possible futures for the children.

I carry the guilt – I feel the shame. I am better than the man who ignored someone suffering. I know I could have done more, but in the end, I did not. Her demons won. I truly hope she ends up in a better place.

I never got to experience life as intended. I never got to experience a marriage built on true love and respect. I am unsure if I ever will, but if I do, you can trust that it is well intended to last. I feel as if I have allowed too much time to pass. That's on me. I also simultaneously believe I have so much love to give. My intention is to give that to someone else.

Time is the one thing we are all running out of. It is consistent and doesn't care who or what you are. Regardless of your desires, it ticks - forging forward whether we want it to or not. Don't waste yours on being a bitter asshole. Be better today and hope to awaken tomorrow. It isn't promised and you will never know the exact time and day it all goes away.

When your Ego

# CHAPTER SIX

## *A SKEPTICS VIEW*

*"Religion is regarded by the common people as true, by the wise as false, and by the rulers as useful."*
Lucius Annaeus Seneca

I understand my religious views do not always correlate well among others. I have my reasons for my beliefs and what I think is an intelligent and scientific example of why I consider myself an Atheist. Yes, I grew up in a few incredibly religious homes. Yes, I was both

When your Ego

baptized and confirmed as a catholic, but this doesn't make me a believer.

My mother was a typical blue collared Italian American Roman catholic. Did she ever have a choice? I am unsure what my father's religion was as a child and into his adult life, but his second marriage moved him into The Mormons. Ah, the good old Church of Jesus Christ of Latter-Day Saints. The LDS, deeply filled with rules and ridiculous assumptions, rumors, jokes, Broadway plays and intrigue.

They forbid or frown upon alcohol, tobacco, coffee, tea, or soda. The demons are introduced into the body with caffeine.

Those are some of their beliefs, and yes, some are health related and very realistic. There are also magic rocks, special underwear, and a questionable debate about paying cash to reach the highest heavens. We haven't even mentioned the theories on women and race, but let's move on before I get myself into trouble.

I am the Outcast member that every family has. While my father did maintain his every other weekend visitation schedule, I am sure he never considered the impact it would have on me religiously. It was never discussed with me by either parent. Regardless, being a child bounced weekly between one belief to the other, didn't take exceptionally long for me to form an opinion.

These two religions had such vast differences that neither could be telling the truth - in my opinion. To be clear, I didn't choose one over the other. The Catholicism was more robotic and old school to me. A complete bore fest but only an hour or less per week. Sit-Stand-Kneel-Pray...Then all your sins are forgiven. What a load of bullshit.

The Mormon part of my life has always been wrapped up in folklore and conspiracies. Their services lasted four plus hours with equal boredom but movement. The message seemed pure, and the people acted sweet and suspiciously innocent in their verbiage and proper dress. Each member referred to others as brothers and sisters. Perhaps not well thought out in a religion based around multiple sex partners.

When your Ego

They treated me no different to my face, but because I wasn't truly one of them, I had alternate rules to abide. I was NOT allowed to be in certain meetings or events. I didn't care very much because none of it interested me as a child.

Most of the Mormon stuff you hear is bullshit. They no longer have multiple wives but from my view they did tend to degrading both women and people of color. It's since loosened up, but my experiences all took place in the late 70's and early 80's. I can't speak of the historical background that formed these seemingly crazy set of rules. I'm not an expert on Mormonism but it's all available online.

Half of my family including my only full sister chose the LDS. They all attended BYU in Utah, and all married within the church. All decent good people and we try not to talk about religious views very often, it rarely turns out well.

I spent more time at LDS temples than most Mormons, but I only got to enter the visitor center. The temples are these large-scale granite fancy gold embossed structures. Money is their motive, as they demand a tithing from every member that equals 15 pct of their yearly earnings. That's a hefty price to pay for absolving your sins, but too each their own. More recently, they have been suspected of some shady money issues. I guess, they are just like every other religion I am aware of - The good, the bad, the ugly and the truth. It seems a lot of demons reside within the believers. Money and greed consume them all.

    My experience with the Mormon church taught me some great, fun life lessons. My first drug experience was with the bishop's son smoking pot at a ward dance that they held monthly. That same dance, I remember David Lee Roth's song California Girls being stopped halfway through because it says, "They keep their boyfriend's warm at night." That was my first experience at censorship.
    A bunch of these kids had alcohol hidden in their pockets and a few of them traveled down bad paths in their future lives. The parents were

When your Ego

completely blinded based solely on their religious teachings. In my parenting experience, the disciplined kids who most imagined would go onto become amazing things, tended to be the ones to indulge negatively once out from their parents' control.

   Mormons, like most religions, highly preach no sex before marriage. It's a nice concept but not able to eliminate the hormones of being a teen. Ironically, Utah has more porn subscriptions per capita than any other state in the United States.
   I touched my first boob and had quite a few innocent touches with many rule abiding Mormon girls. It was a mostly fun and a non-religious time among the children. None of them seemed to care what my beliefs were. Most of them had little choice or options in their own beliefs and have grown to become amazing people. Also, many that I knew have decided to leave the church.
   The" Magic underwear" or temple garments internally referred as, always made me smile.

My father had them and they resembled a unitard for men. The brief history of them is meant as a reminder to their promises and covenants made with God. To me it is not much different from other religious garments.

The sexuality involved between two consenting members can be dicey. The funniest part about it is how the college aged horny little believers have found a way around the rules.

"SOAKING"- *soaking refers to penetration, but no thrusting, which makes the act not fornication, and thus not requiring a bishop's interview. It's an LDS version of the old "just the tip" excuse.*

In my personal experience I think I would rather NOT get laid. The thought of being inside a willing participant and just lying there without movement seems daunting. Sex should never be a non-contact activity. I have too many questions concerning this, and I intend to find a willing partner to experiment with this activity. This is for research purposes only.

When your Ego

On the catholic end, that's where much of my upbringing and teaching remained. I also had little choices and was forced into the biblical hell of CCD. I barely had the energy for regular school, and I had no interest in learning about religion. My mind just didn't see the same visions. I saw bullshit - I saw so many story holes in their theory.

Later in life, I am enthralled in people who wrap their lives around any belief. I thoroughly enjoy educational documentaries involving beliefs throughout the world. I am never disrespectful toward those who choose to believe. I understand the comfort it can bring to someone thinking that when you die, there is a place to see your loved ones again.

As an Atheist, I simply live my life thinking and being conscious to always try and be a decent human. I do believe in karma, but I just cannot wrap my head around an invisible man in the sky. The truth is that neither of us really know. I prefer to think that the light you see at the end of the tunnel when you die, is you being born and reentered. It isn't necessarily a belief, but more of a wish. Anything to get a second chance to get this life thing right.

    I once visited my priest at his home beside the church. He answered the door in a "Grab a Heine" T-shirt that was a popular advert for Heineken beer. He invited me in when I requested to ask him a question. I had inquired about seeing images of my grandmother after her death. He listened and thought about it before giving me some bullshit answer. I didn't understand his answer but because I was taught to trust my teachers, priests, and adults - I never considered him feeding me garbage.
    After an hour, he had talked me into smoking pot with him. We stood behind his house mere feet from the home of Jesus, puffing on a rolled joint like two teens behind the school. Because of my trust, I didn't think this was anything wrong. It oddly made me see him as the flawed human he was - rather than the projected voice of God that my mother had told me he was.

When your Ego

My priest didn't harm me or try to molest me. He was charged with such crimes later, but with me it was only smoking pot. I jokingly used to ask, "why not me - am I not attractive?" But I learned over time that it is nothing to joke about. My inappropriate jokes are common and often used to deflect.

Eventually, I was caught by him stealing the Eucharist from backstage behind the altar. Turns out they come in big plastic bulk bags and really don't have any taste. I suppose if all the after-death hub bub is true, I am bound for hell. I am fairly sure stealing from a church is an automatic dismissal from heaven. If all of it is true - I will suffer the consequences. I am sure a few of my friends will be waiting.

My first example of non-belief, of course began with the two religions saying two different things. The second was at around age twelve. My grandmother who we called mum, a sweet and amazing woman who watched endless hours of nuns on television, would often let me know that if I am bad - I will go to hell. She wasn't being mean - she honestly believed and lived her life by her beliefs. And I was a punk. A bad mischievous asshole with a mouth to match. The problem I had was why is going to hell a dreadful thing? My theories said if I am bad and hell or the devil are bad - why would he punish me? Wouldn't he worship me and want me?

   I didn't have the courage to ever bring my thoughts up to my parents. They both believed so deeply that I had little chance of being acknowledged as correct. Later in life, I did bring my theory up to my father. To his credit - he didn't dismiss it. He had an answer that made some sense. Not completely, but it was intelligent and civil. He said his version of hell is not necessarily the flames and the burning, but rather the pain is like a window where you can endlessly watch your loved ones happily together in heaven. You have no contact, and they can't see you. I admit - that's painful. Unfortunately for me, I still can't wrap my head around this heaven stuff.

   Several years ago, when my daughter was around eight, she attended a friend's mother's

When your Ego

funeral. This was her first church experience since I obviously never preached any opinion on religion - including my own. As we sat surrounded by loved ones and their families, the priest began his rehearsed mantra of the wine and bread. He raised the wafer above his head and proclaimed, "this is my body etc., etc." I am not able to verse it verbatim but if you know you know. He then lifted his golden chalice and once again proclaimed, "this is my blood" Well that was all she needed to hear. As he sipped from the cup, she yelled out - "oh my god he is drinking blood." The poor kid was traumatized and luckily most within earshot found her comment hilarious.

Throughout the years as a non-believer, I never pushed my agenda or beliefs on anyone - including my kids. If the subject comes up, I discuss my argument but only if the person or people are willing to remain civil. The truth is no one truly knows what will happen. My family is filled with amazing people who happen to strongly believe. They respect my opinion in front of me, but I am sure behind my back I am spoken of. I am the lesser child - the black cloud. I am also the least educated and the poorest.

My remaining issues are arguments around the terrible things. How an all-loving god creates murders and missing or exploited children. How planes crash and good decent humans die of suffering disease. Why is molestation so rampant within the religions? Why are the bad people living into their later lives? And why is my mother dead?

I have a lot of questions about a subject that I am not willing to accept. I often said, "When my mom appears and hands me a twenty-dollar bill - I will believe"

The only argument I find myself in with my siblings is my lack of visiting my mother's grave. I usually have a gas lighting response arguing that if they believe what they preach, then why can't I just visit her in my living room. It's a dickish response and one I need to be less aggressive with. My mother was a good woman and deserves my attention - believer or not - as a respectful gesture for the life she led. I owe her that.

I honestly have no disrespect or issue with your believing. All that I ask, as an Atheist, is not that you believe in my opinion but that you believe that I believe my opinions. It's all mutual respect and truthfully none of us know where or what happens when we die.

**JUST A NOTE:**

I do feel that religion drove a stake between my father and me. I don't doubt his strong belief but do struggle with that his religion always was more important than I was. Although, my son being gay was a huge issue to him, both morally and religiously, he manages to accept my son in the family. I personally don't believe he really does fully accept, but I appreciate his efforts to not make things uncomfortable. He is a proud and amazing man regardless.

The truth may never be known. I will never say my father doesn't love me, but he loves his beliefs much more. At this point, he is very elderly and in good health. We both seem to have chosen to enjoy what we have left and accept or ignore the differences between us both. One day after his passing, I will reflect on the good times and review the bad. In the end, he is my father, and I wouldn't change a thing about him.

**FINAL NOTE:**

Life is confusing enough. Once you inject religion into the mix, prepare for a bumpy ride. I'm not alone and many remain disconnected and unwilling to accept a differing opinion. It isn't only religion, but politics and parenting styles could become endless arguments without an end. I won't be that type of Son. He is my father

When your Ego

and I love him for all the flaws he has and can only hope he also has a similar thinking.

The conversations we engage in now are far more enjoyable. We have settled the differences with both of us being respectful and silent about the words that once hurt us both. We both have grown. The past is over but not unrepaired. I am proud of us both.

When your Ego

# CHAPTER SEVEN

## *THE SUICIDE EFFECT*

*"The obsession with suicide is characteristic of the man who can neither live nor die, and whose attention never swerves from this double impossibility."*
Emil Cioran

Suicide has played a consistent role in my lifetime. Whether a planned attempt of my own, which never has been implemented, or the many unfortunate connections who succeeded. I have never spoken of my own darkness and the plan I had in place. It was altered and well thought out throughout the years whenever a new dark period arrived. I must admit, the dark times seemed more frequent in my younger years. I suppose that experience, numbness and understanding that the option isn't the solution grows with each passing year. But it hasn't disappeared.

Now this isn't a cry for help or a threat. It is simply a moment of exposing my identity. It isn't a comfortable moment, or a weight lifted from my back. Some feel relief when they declare themselves incapable of and solve the issues by revealing them to the world. I don't. I wish I did. I am a huge fan and often support anyone asking for help. There is a subtle bravery in being able to be strong enough to show a weakness. Before I dive into my personal plan, let me go back to the first instance of suicide that affected me.

When your Ego

    Trudging up the steep hill home from school was a daunting task on its own. For Greg it included a daily fight for his perceived survival. He was considered as being different - whatever that means - between ten-year-olds. A typical response by others often resulted in bullying tactics. I am included, although I have no true memory of causing any physical harm. Mostly, I simply watched as others teased, tripped, punched, and kicked him. I didn't protect him in any way.
    I often joined in on the ridicule. The mental breakdown that separated his ability to walk to school safely. The name calling always feels innocent when you are a child. Turns out, often, it matters. This kid never had a chance. His torture never ended.


    Mental health had zero mentions through my childhood. It was approaching the eighties but the gender roles remained antiquated and slowly moving toward where they stand today. If boys cried, they were weak and often threatened by the adults. We were told to fight and be strong. "Never let them see you cry." It was a constant dose of toxic masculinity cast upon us kids. We learned to hold in all our emotions and that's what we mostly remain today.

What no one ever knew was that Greg's beating continued once he was home. The one place every child should be guaranteed safety was no more than more bruising. It may have been worse, but no one knew - no one could see behind his walls.

After receiving a poor grade on his report card. He attempted to change the grade and was caught. After the teachers told him that his parents were being contacted, he went home, loaded a rifle, and wrote a note. Sadly, he did tell others of his plan on his way home. One brave kid called 911 and the police arrived at his house. They determined that Greg was calm and polite. He told them it was a hoax and they dismissed it as such. As they pulled away, Greg placed that note on the table, put the gun to his mouth and fired.

## When your Ego

Later in my life, and a year after my divorce, another suicide incident changed my world. I didn't know the man and had no friendship with him. His reason written was me.

I had met a girl at the local bar. We instantly connected and began a short whirlwind romance that lasted nine days. On the 8th day, we made plans to bar hop and go wherever the evening would take us. One bar turned into five, and my mind spun as we consistently downed every shot.

The girl had brought along her roommate. He was a soft-spoken man in his 30's and broke. I ended up paying for his evening and he easily kept up with every shot. The two of them indulged in other powdery substances and eventually we all ended up at their house - continuing the party.

Everyone was drunk. Soon, a sibling-like argument between them broke out. They began physically pushing one another, but it never transpired further. After a bit of loud shouting and idle threats, the two of them separated. He went to his room, and we went to hers. It was now nearing 3 am, and a loud hammering on the wall behind her headboard woke us. She jumped out of bed and another brief argument ensued. I listened through the doorway as he explained an inability to sleep and decided to hang some pictures on his wall.

    She returned enraged and then we all fell asleep.

    The following late morning, we awoke. I dragged my tired hungover ass to the car, and we headed out for breakfast and shopping. At the end of the afternoon, I dropped her off at home and picked up my toddler daughter. My phone was ringing as I entered my house.

    "Hello," I said.

    "Something here isn't right," she whispered.

    Her voice trembled and she spoke softly as she approached her third floor door. I heard her unlock it and walk in calling his name.

    "What's wrong?" I asked.

        She was immediately spooked and made her way back down the stairs and out toward her car.

When your Ego

"Can you come by?"
I hung up and got my young daughter into the car. She only lived a few blocks away, so I arrived at her quickly. She slumped sadly while smoking and shaking beside her car.
"What's the problem?"
"It's after 3 and he should be at work. His car is still here."
"Well, maybe he slept in."

I took her keys and went up to her apartment while her and my daughter stayed outside. The door opened to her kitchen, and I called out his name. No response. When I got to his door, I knocked lightly and turned the knob. I knew before it was opened. I could see his shadow and the air was different.
It turns out that his picture hanging was nails into the closet header. He then stripped down to his boxers, removed all his jewelry and placed it beside the note on his bed. With his leather belt, he created a noose and lifted his feet from the floor. When I found him, his feet dragged beneath him with his knee's mere

inches from the floor. A lot of the blood had rushed to his feet, and they had swollen unbelievably.

Once the police arrived, my ex-wife picked up my daughter. I wasn't present then and my memories may differ from the reality. What I do remember is feeling guilt. I had no idea that he had feelings toward his roommate and that he had finally reached the edge. When I spoke with the police, they informed me how lucky I am. They said that usually in these situations, they take out their competition before ending their lives. I spent countless nights reliving the opportunity that he had.

I was drunk and passed out no more than ten feet away. Her door was unlocked, and I would have never felt his presence. I've woken up in night sweats dreaming of this nightmare. I didn't know him - but I could see his face as if I had known him my whole life. I also treated him nicely. I like to believe that this is the reason I am alive today.

That relationship ended before it could begin.

## When your Ego

About a year after the incident, I did something that I am not immensely proud to have done. While racked and suffering with guilt, I disguised myself as an interviewer and scheduled a meeting with the deceased man's mother. She agreed and we spoke of loss and unanswered questions. I brought this innocent woman back to those days, and I did it for selfish reasons.

She divulged the information in his note. She called it that, but it may have been something either sent to her prior or left on the scene. Hearing her mention my likeness made it difficult to remain anonymous. I fought through revealing my actual self and thanked her for her honesty. She also told me about missing items and continued usage of his AOL INTERNET account. I was no part of any thefts or the AOL usage. All that I could say is that I have learned and have grown immensely since that unknown man took his life.

**FINAL NOTES:**

The next chapter I will delve deeper into my own dark moments. I had a few months between writing this part because I am nervous about the impact on my children. After careful consideration, this story could only help myself and others.

I am NOT alone but sometimes I still feel I am. We can all benefit from hearing some truths.

When your Ego

# CHAPTER EIGHT

## *FIND ME IN THE DARKNESS*

At one point or another, we all have spent time in the darkness. Some have the external support to overcome it, but far too many are alone in their struggle. I never felt the support, but I also didn't ever ask or reveal any of my thoughts.

I didn't grow up in poverty – I didn't ever need to know where my next meal would come from. I never went to sleep in my car or didn't have an

When your Ego

opportunity to educate myself. So where does suicide ideation become an everyday process?

   For anyone triggered by discussions involving suicide. This chapter may NOT be for you. I have chosen to detail my ideations in hopes of helping others understand them and find their way to a happy and productive life.

   Being affected at an early age with issues intended for older people to deal with may have excelled the thoughts. Being sexually molested or simply just trying to exist could have impacted me in ways I never known. Or it may just be inside me, lurking, hidden, waiting to take control. The point may be that some of us just have a mental trajectory without any catalytic event. Human wiring is an intricate and awkward thing to understand.

   I've never spoken to someone about my darkness. When I say no one, I mean this is my first time ever attempting to say it aloud. For far too long, I hid my truth behind a shell protected by comedic remarks and replies of, "I'm doing great." Followed by something productive that I've completed.

All lies.

Suicide ideation is the consideration that killing myself is always an option. I have been lucky enough to discuss the affliction with other people who have been guests on my mental health podcast – Happy Hour with Scott H. Silverman. Unfortunately, I wasn't being honest when I inquired about their ideations while pretending to not know what they were speaking about.

If you listen back, you can hear me deflect it away from me. My questions are less than what I may normally ask on the show– because I already knew the answers.

One guy specifically sticks in my memory. Frank King, who is a mental health comedian and six-time TED Talk participant, joined Scott Silverman and me to discuss his life. He simplified the definition of suicide ideation, which

When your Ego

he has dealt with all his life and is well educated on its impact.

Frank said, "most people when their car breaks down have the option to A. buy a new car B. call a tow truck. But, with suicide ideation there is a third option. You can kill yourself and solve the problem."

He continued to explain how every problem in his life has that third option. Obviously, he hasn't done it, but the thought is still present. I found it fascinating when explained in simple terms.

I should let you know that my personal issues with suicide ideation took place from about ten years old and well into my thirties. I've since grappled with the past, challenged myself to figure out the issues, and conquer them the best way I could.

The problem with telling people that now is that I have exposed myself and presented a confession as a liar. Just a few paragraphs ago, I explained that my, "I'm doing fine." – and my, "I'm good." Was all utter bullshit. So how can I say the same thing now and make you believe that I am?

I guess you can assume that I am alive and breathing at fifty-four years old or that my past examples of telling the brutal and honest truth in this book, could help. You could believe me without comment, or you could remain a skeptic in my admissions. Having authored several books has blessed me with thickened skin. I am unafraid of these opinions. I wouldn't ever keep trying to tell my stories if the ridicule and negativity affected me.

The use of "affected me greatly" is an interesting phrase. It's vague and all telling simultaneously. it deserves further analysis. I am an approval junkie who wants everyone to like or love me. I need to be recognized and approved by the masses to feel verified or alive. It is a shallow and sometimes aggressive form of "look at me – am I good enough yet?"

This isn't some made up diagnosis and mine specifically isn't therapist diagnosed. If you listen to Dax Shepard on his podcast of which I am a

When your Ego

huge fan, he often mentions that he is an addict and an approval junkie.

APPROVAL JUNKIE - *An approval addict is someone who relies on the approval of others for their self-esteem and self-worth. Much like a people pleaser, approval addicts fear rejection, judgment, or disapproval from others to the point that they try to avoid rocking the boat at all costs.*

Now that the definition is here, I see some stark opposites that I portray. The word "relies" seems to mean at no end. I do NOT rely on it, but I purposely seek it. The fear of rejection fits and is my most common attribute to not completing a project. The next line, "avoids rocking the boat" is quite the opposite for me. I adopted the phrase and flipped it, just to use it as a deflection mechanism. I often play devil's advocate and ask tough questions. On my podcast A DUDE IN THE HENHOUSE – I often argue from a place of getting the truth. This fucking flaw results in most people disliking me well before they like me. I'd love to say it's an act, but it's an unfortunate built in response to any question.

   I am usually not seeking an argument, rather, I'm looking to figure out all sides of the debate. I am genuinely interested in all angles. I tend to over think. I am well planned and deliberate with always knowing where the exit is. And I always find the negative before the positive. I highly doubt my own abilities and I am quick to celebrate another's. I have a few flaws remaining to be explored or are under repair.

   Back to the darkness –

   The following few paragraphs I will attempt to describe my plan. It isn't easy, nor is it enjoyable. I hope that it is helpful. My darkness isn't yours, and yours isn't mine.

   I never had a sleepover as a child. Very few friends ever entered my house. We never spent

When your Ego

summer days playing baseball in my yard. I have singular amazing memories of my childhood, unlike other kids with many.

   I didn't understand the darkness, but it still found me when I was young. It wasn't some monster in the closet or under my bed. It was living inside of me, gnawing at my insides, and whispering in my ear whenever I closed my eyes to sleep.

   I was ten years old when I found the gun. It was tucked into the back of the desk drawer, hidden in a large calculator pleather case. The handle fit well in my hands as I studied it from all angles. Five small shiny bullets sat in the bottom of the case and stared back at me. One copper colored tip was visible when I investigated the barrel.

   Everything I am typing I didn't remember until this moment. I never imagined dredging up forgotten memories and telling them to the world. All of it is overwhelming and helpful. All of it has flooded back.

I thought about initially wounding myself and getting the pity. I figured that a suicide attempt would get them to get me help. I was ten and had no reason to even know what suicide was about. I remember thinking that someone would care. Someone would ask me questions and reveal the inside monsters attacking me.

I ended up putting it all back and closing the drawer, but I knew where it was. I knew when the time was right, I could revisit. This is when my over thinking brain may have saved me. Although, looking down at the barrel of a loaded gun, it's lucky enough that no accidents occurred.

I was clearly carrying guilt from the sexual molestation and holding it in had become taxing. I just wasn't happy. Knowing that my loss would affect my mother's life, kept me from revisiting the gun. A few years later if my memory serves me, I sold the gun to a neighbor. Now I realize the severity and future harm this act could have caused. I hadn't understood that as a child.

When your Ego

Only two teachers in my life recognized issues. Mrs. Harlow, a local and often utilized substitute teacher had once inquired with me privately about my home life. I lied and manipulated my way through it all. In the early eighties teachers had less power to make educated accusations.

The other teacher was in Middle School and often butted heads with me because I was a wiseass little fucker. Mr. Harrison took the ridicule well but wasn't out of line when he asked me about my home life. Once again, I wiggled out of it.

Both teachers still managed to temporarily change my path. Just caring at all was enough to keep me going.

My teen years brought out an angrier inside young man. I was transferred from my mother's home to my father's, and he moved me to my uncle's. I was merely a thirteen-year-old package sent to the wrong address. I had no voice to where I lived, but my uncle's house was a wonderful opportunity to breathe.

This was the safest option barring the neighborhood. In this home I seemed to matter. I had a voice to make my own decisions and I felt happy. Perhaps, too much freedom, but it felt good to control the path. Outside the safe walls of my new home, race relations and criminal activities posed a challenge. I had never had to deal with race issues. It only takes a few lost fights and punches to your head before you learn the rules. I learned them swiftly.

Once I learned the rules, I began to run the streets. My comfort level and freedom created an updated version of myself, hellbent on being self-destructing. The drinking began, the smoking began, the drugs emerged and conquered. It was a fast-paced gradual movement into nightly debauchery, and a lot of fun until it wasn't.

I was over my head. Hanging mostly late night with most friends being significantly older. My tolerance increased and my demons started to rise. Alcohol and girls fueled the anger and my past. Eventually the summer was over, and my first year began. I chose Platt tech vs the

When your Ego

local high school. My oldest sister, a star student, had just graduated prior to me entering. I assume they thought, "how amazing to get the brother of an amazing student." Unfortunately, the answer appeared quickly.

"Not lucky at all."

I never found my place in high school. From day one I was lost in a sea of cliques and unknown fellow students from neighboring towns I never knew existed. The rules of high school didn't fit well into my introvert until an extrovert way, and I would be suspended too many times to count. Within year two or my second first year, they requested me to take my future elsewhere. Upon not taking their hint, I was politely told not to return. I never saw most of those friends again.

My uncle tired of my attitude and I was moved back to my father's. All was fine and the comfort level was tolerable. No one ever asked if I needed help. No one checked in on my schooling. No one had any time between work and the new baby sister who arrived.

My father walked me into my first day at West haven high school. We sat with the counselor who instructed me to the office to get my schedule. My father stayed behind. I walked past the office, out the front door and watched as my father drove away. I never spent a single minute inside a classroom and skipped class for four months before anyone noticed. I am unsure if this was about my father or the school, but what I realized was that no one had my best interest in their mind. If I was going to survive, it had to be on me.

I failed out of another high school, all before completing the ninth grade. That was the last level of education I would receive. It had nothing to do with being dumb or smart. It had little to do with the studies or the schools. I wish I could have an answer to why I didn't matter.

My insides hurt with deep internal failures. I never wanted to end up a drop out but never had the voice to ask for help. Truly little of this could fall on my parents. I know plenty of other kids who had similar issues in their home lives,

When your Ego

many of them still succeeded. This is partly why I often tell new parents that they have little control of the outcome.

   I prefer to take the blame. I never let my shield down and they never saw through my deflection. If you lived in the seventies or eighty's, the parenting style was different. Very few parents knew where the kids were at until after that Adam Walsh kid went missing from a mall. The world had extraordinarily little mental health awareness and google didn't exist.

   The convenience of blaming my parents existed until I became a parent. I felt like an active parent and my kids still slipped past my eyeline. I constantly see amazing parents with horrible children, and then horrible parents with amazing kids. I have little choice but to consider how little it matters beyond the typical rules of law and politeness. Maybe I'm wrong, but we all have seen this pattern continue for centuries.

   My first real suicide attempt was developed out in a plan. My metal band BORN DEAD was filling my time and my lyrics were written around death & dying. I needed to find a way to disappear and not be found by anyone. I preferred my parents thinking I just walked away and could be fine vs. seeing my body dangling from a noose. I had way too much vanity to put a bullet through my head, and pills or drowning didn't impress me.

I began to study the trains and their schedules. I never considered the life altering vision of the train engineer watching it in real time. The plan was to do it on a late rainy night with the thought that any blood would get washed away. I imagined a train would hit me and I would disappear into thin air. This plan eliminated when a family friend named Palmer inadvertently died while playing chicken on the train tracks. His mother chose an open casket to show his friends what drugs could lead you into – it worked for me.

Long story short – the band broke up. I gave up on music as a career and shifted my life towards girls. I was approaching the summer of 1986 and seventeen. This is when I met the girl.

When your Ego

I don't recall the first meeting, but I imagine it took place at the Milford mall or Milford rec. I don't recall if I was instantly interested, but I imagine that I was. I managed to somehow, through relationships and marriage, to always think she was the one who got away.

She isn't aware, unless she reads my book – that without her I am not here. Her friendship, memory and brief interlude of sexual exploration injected a positivity that never escaped my head.

We were merely kids from different sides of town. It predated social media, so we spent our apart time on the phone. We connected. We had similarities and we enjoyed each other's company when together. Unfortunately, it just never became more. Our friendship remains and the respect is mutually strong. What happens in the future I can't predict, but without her I am not the same man.

I know it isn't typical to meet and hold onto a wish for forty years, but this is a book of truths. because I already spoke of this woman earlier in the book, I don't feel it needs repeating.

I spent the next few years working shitty jobs – moving from home to home and eventually sleeping outside the local diner at the truck stop because I had nowhere else to go. Eventually I found a decent job and got my own apartment.

July 21, 1987, was a Tuesday. It remains engrained forever in my memory. The weather was summer perfect, and the McDonalds parking lot was humming with a gaggle of horny teens with no ability to vote. The cool kids and the wannabes all harmoniously gathered in their cliques and did their thing. Everyone had different musical styles and they often competed by trying to overpower the others' music.

The metal heads usually won. Being A much more powerful and consistent speed that rose above the rest. It was not a taste for everyone but on this night it did not matter. On this night, everyone was listening to the same album.

The sun had just set, and the parking lot was more active than normal. I saw people attempting to synchronize together their car

When your Ego

speakers to make each song that much louder. It didn't really work. Back then we could only press play and pray. We lacked the technology that our kids are blessed with today.

    I stood in the far corner with my everyday crew – smoking Marlboro cigarettes and touching my hair. We also had the same album on repeat and really enjoyed the songs that grabbed our attention. The only problem was that everyone else's attention was circling near the McDonald's entrance. We headed toward the crowd to make sure we didn't miss anything because the fear of missing out was built into our DNA.

    The crowd swayed and moved. I squeezed my then much thinner frame between the crowd and witnessed what I hope to see again one day. It resembled seeing my favorite band or kissing that girl at a party. It was magical.

    Standing on the plastic tables, with a portable tape player blaring a new song titled Mr. Brownstone, were the girls from our clique dancing like strippers at a nightclub. My focus went directly to them all as they wildly put on a show. Denise led the routine which makes sense. But once I spotted her, my one and only, I was sure to burn the image into my brain.

She looked amazing with her tiny little ass shaking in her marginally tight blue jeans. Her white tee shirt with a black bra strap visible near her neckline. She wasn't a center of attention type but tonight she danced carefree. I never took my eyes off her and I don't think she saw me watching. I think she may have been transported to another place, as we all seemed to whenever Guns and Roses songs came on.

Our brief teenage existence all went away in a blink. I disappeared and only with the invention of social media, I was found once again. All the friends except a few moved on. Some of them made it out while others met tragic ends. I never got to properly say goodbye to that girl, and I can only hope that she knows her role in saving my life.

It all happens so fast. The memories fade away and get replaced by others as we age. The mall isn't the same and the arcade has long

When your Ego

since been destroyed. McDonald's remains but Walmart has replaced the trailer park in the woods across the road. There's no more crazy bread and cheap liquor poured into soda cups, but I will never forget the look in her eye as she danced on July 21$^{st}$ in the summer of 1987.

The last time I considered suicide as an option was at the age of thirty-five. My life was not going as planned. My marriage had failed, and my drinking was becoming a daily activity. I was sad. The girl I wanted was in the past but not forgotten. She found her path and married another. I always just wanted her to be happy.

It's strange to me that while being unhappy, I still rooted for everyone else. I've always been a better support to others rather than to myself. I had so many dreams go up in smoke and I finally reached a level of fuck it – go die already.

I devised a plan. I thought it through and considered my children carefully. I really thought they wouldn't miss me. I threw a full raging pity party and invited no one to the event. I wrote and edited my suicide note. A sad and ridiculous letter blaming everyone except myself. It took about a week before I intended to complete the task.

This time I wasn't messing around. I bought a handgun off the New Haven streets and one single bullet to fit. I doubled down with enough liquor to down a horse and topped it with street purchased pills that I knew wouldn't mix well with alcohol added. I had a checklist of goodbyes, including that girl. I began saying my goodbyes prior to when I took my children for the weekend. They didn't know it was farewell.

When the day arrived, I woke up like every other day. I ate breakfast, had coffee, and studied my list for any missed errors. I called my mother to her surprise. We spoke for a bit until she had to leave. I picked up the phone to call the girl but paused when considering her current relationship. I assumed she was incredibly happy, and I didn't ever want her to feel guilty or haunted by talking to me. Everything was in place. Nothing was missing. I hand wrote my suicide note and laid it on my dresser. At the

When your Ego

same time, I removed the gun and the bullet before walking to the kitchen table. I placed it to my dominant left side for quicker access.

    I knew I was stalling. Even though I planned this perfectly, something still whispered in my ear. I poured my first drink at ten in the morning and continued to drink one after the next. I kept writing on my tablet about movie ideas that I had never begun.

    When I looked up it was ten in the evening. No one had called me. No one stopped by. I had two more hours to complete the task and all my problems would go away. It really felt that easy.

    By eleven at night, I was ready. It was raining outside, and I opened the window. I was thinking that if I weren't found for a while the smell would be less with fresh air blowing through. I poured a final tall glass of rum with coke with a single ice cube left in the tray. I locked my door.

    The TV was on ESPN – The Red Sox had won, and I smiled. I was far beyond drunk and could barely focus on the screen. Once I took the final sip of my drink – I grabbed the gun and practiced angles of where to fire it. I kept thinking through the temple but then settled on under my jawline. Once I put the tip on my skin, I paused to say, "I am sorry."

    The single bullet was just out of arm's length, so I stood to grab it. Between my nerves and my drunkenness, I fumbled it and it fell to the floor. I tried to stand to flip on the light switch, but the table was my only crutch. I simply laid my head on the kitchen table and awoke with an unbelievably bad headache the next morning. I failed, but this time my failure saved me.

    I had to fill in a lot of holes here to make this readable. Some may be dramatized, and some could be false. When I say I was drunk, I was hammered beyond the limits. When I said I wanted to die, I meant it. All the events are true. As a writer of fiction, I easily could have fired the unloaded gun to draw in the suspense. My point in this description is to show the fear existed. I never intended to describe the dead set truth of that day, but my intentions were to give examples of survival. I delayed, waited, killed

When your Ego

time. At any point I could have taken the pills and ended it by falling asleep. Instead, I wrote.

Writing could be a strong therapist. If I didn't have it, my life would be completely changed. It's partly why I can manage a bad book review, because I author the book for me. Every story I tell has pieces of me intertwined within its depths. All my stories have a character somewhere contemplating the end. And a shameless plug – all my books are available on Amazon.

Maybe if we adjust our efforts with calls or drop ins to those who may be struggling. I don't know if it would have changed my mind, but it would have given me time. When someone reaches the point I reached, nothing deters the process. But we can try to learn how to be more aware. Maybe then we can change the course.

**FINAL NOTES:**

Sometimes I repeat myself and I am enthusiastic toward solving mental health and suicidal issues. The world has changed since I was a young man, but in some ways social media has helped and harmed the causes. It's time to be the nosey parent. Be like me and dig deep into things and discover the truth. My kids got away with plenty, but I made it my job to analyze the unimportant things.

We judge others harshly. We always think everyone is showing us the complete story. We always have an opinion. The problem is that we aren't listening to hear, we are listening to respond. Maybe if a few of us stop pretending that everything will be all right, we could change the narrative. Suicide prevention should be a concern. One day it will be someone you care about deeply.

When your Ego

# CHAPTER NINE

## *DREAM CHASING*

Through all my early life struggles, I never allowed my dreams to die. I had no one in my family interested in film, but when my father took me at way too young an age to see Close Encounters of the Third Kind, I believe the dream began. (I was eight.)

Star Wars arrived a few months prior, but I don't remember it impacting me the same. In those six months I matured. What I do remember about Star Wars was the action. I

When your Ego

don't mean the action on the screen, but rather the fight my stepfather got into with the people in front of us.

Now being merely eight, I didn't understand film making. At the time Steven Spielberg was only 30 and this was his first film since his breakout JAWS.  The shark film hadn't been on my radar yet and once it was, even my swimming pool activities were forgotten.

PG 13 didn't exist. Either your parents took you to the theater or you turned 17 and could go on your own to a restricted rated film. The sneak in happened from time to time, but usually we were caught before the film had begun. HBO existed but no one had it, and once we did have cable television, there was no way our working-class parents were paying for it. If you had HBO, you would be living the dream.

**On a side note** – I can remember seeing HBO for the first time with my young eyes.  It was a sleepover birthday and I was eleven. My old-time friend Jimmy Goldbeck had it and FLASH GORDON was the film that I saw. I remember thinking, "no commercials?" as I chose to watch it the rest of the night.

   Now that my love of film has been born. I immersed myself deeply, finding opportunities to discover my niche. It began with the non-cable UHF channels that often played old black and white movies. KING KONG – GODZILLA – WESTERNS among many others. There wasn't HD and your signal could become unstable. It didn't matter. And then the VCR appeared in my teen years.
   There just was so much to choose from once the invention of video stores arrived. BLOCKBUSTER VIDEO was the big boy but there were mom and pop versions that popped into every strip mall. It worked similarly to a Library where if you had the club card you could rent any available movie for a low-cost price. It truly was a weekend event.
   Before I captivate you with my love of all things JOHN HUGHES, let me help you understand the real people who formed my cinephile desires.

When your Ego

I began with all the typical films of my age and genre. E.T. – INDIANA JONES - and at the time – bad <u>STAR WARS</u>.  Unfortunately, I fell into the years of the prequels. They weren't unwatchable, it's still Star Wars, but some of the choices weren't exactly cinematic gems and never came close to the first three released.

E.T. mattered deeply to me. It's one of the first films to feel as if it was written for me. The misunderstood young boy Eliott who no one believes. You had divorced parents and the BMX bikes, and the bikes play a role in my story.

It was my main mode of transportation. Our parents rarely knew or cared we went. On a specific day when my mother was taking my little sister to see the film, I took a summer road trip with my biker gang.

It all began innocently and quickly became a dare. "Whoever can cross the train tracks on their bike closest to the moving train – wins."

I do not know who stated the dare, but when you are twelve – you accept it.

Some of my friends had higher end bikes – I had a Huffy with very few add on accessories. It didn't matter, I needed to win. We could feel the vibrations as another train approached. Many in the group either crossed to the other side before the train was visible or chickened out altogether. Me with my never ending need to fit in, chose an extremely late start and struggled to bunny hop the tracks. By the time I had crossed I could feel the trains suction on my back. If I had failed or wasted a single second – this book would have ended in 1982.

Fortunately, I survived and won. Unfortunately, the Milford police were waiting on the side I was on. A bunch of my friends scattered in different directions, just like we planned for this event. I was trapped and gave myself up. They quickly removed me from the tracks and questioned my stupidity.

Before cellphones, getting ahold of a parent was not an easy task. Why I decided to tell them the truth about my mom's whereabouts baffles me to this day. The Police contacted the theater,

When your Ego

they then stopped the movie to call out her name – and she jokingly would mention that she never saw the ending of E.T.

Let the John Hughes era begin.

"You See Us as You Want to See Us, In the Simplest Terms with The Most Convenient Definitions. But What We Found Out Is That Each One of Us Is a Brain... And An Athlete... And A Basket Case...

I am a John Hughes junkie. Ever since those five students arrived for Saturday detention, my heart has felt so full. It wasn't one specific character, but rather the whole fucking cast. I found a piece of me in them all.
THE BREAKFAST CLUB hit me where it healed.

<u>John Bender</u> – The Rebel - his home life being imperfect. He uses a false shield of toughness to deflect his real pain.

Claire – The Princess – Her home life is less than stellar. She conforms to the needs of others just to fit into her clique.

Allison – The Outcast – Hidden in silence behind her pain. She tells lies to impress when she just wants to be liked.

Brian – The Brain – The pressures of being a student his overwhelming his life causing the thoughts of suicide.

Andrew – The Jock – Never feeling he is enough to satisfy his father, he uses bullying tactics to gain attention.

No singular person stands out more than the next. I compare pieces of them all. The antics of the film do NOT all age well in the current world, but the message still exists. This is when I thought my career would be in film.

I never told my film plans to anyone. I began studying dialogue and watching films from different perspectives. Unfortunately, my cinephile mental madness has created a pattern.

When your Ego

I want most films, the good and the bad, at least three times.
One time for entertainment.
The second time for dialogue and transitions.
The third time for Camera angles and lighting.

It's completely mental but this far into the book, nothing should shock you now.

I can ramble on about the genius of Cameron Crowe. His film ALMOST FAMOUS captured the life he lived and the life I wanted. His use of characters, and dialogue – makes me feel weepy inside. He touches my soul with most endeavors he approaches. His personality shines through the music, and his talent grasps the power of words. ELIZABETHTOWN is a highly underrated film in my opinion. JERRY MAGUIRE and FAST TIMES AT RIDGEMONT HIGH – to name a few. Let me know what you think?

I genuinely believe that I could see a movie every day in the theater. I never miss the coming soon trailers and if I do, it ruins the film I am watching. I often go alone.

Some people question how I do this all alone but it's a film – I am not here to chit chat. Places I don't enjoy on my own are museums and art galleries. They deserve an opinionated debate and I really enjoy that.

Most of my greatest memories involve a movie. I believe in love because of it – even if I understand the unrealistic story, I still believe. I talk about fictional characters as if they are real people. I understand storylines and occasionally side with the bad guy. Whenever someone starts a conversation about movies, I instantly perk up with joy.

My Christmas day always includes a theater visit. I am not Jewish, but I do believe I deserve an honorary membership into their club. I even eat Chinese for dinner before shutting off my Christmas lights and turning in.

That's the one thing my life is missing. A good Christmas day. It weighs on me so deeply that I

When your Ego

imagine my film will include a man in search of the holiday. I know poor Fredd has shitty Christmas's – just another pity cast upon him. Let's get back to my dream.

My dream of making a film was paused when I became a single dad. I know I made the correct choice, but I regret not following through with the dream. I never stopped writing. All my books are written as screenplays, albeit very rough drafts. Now that I am older and an empty nester, the movie dream has reawakened. I will make at least one film in my lifetime. And if I die before I get the chance – tell my kids to film my funeral and release it in my name. They can pick the title.

**FINAL NOTES:**

Chase your dream and never stop. You get this one singular life, so fuck what the critics may say. I allowed a lifestyle shift to kill mine off and I regret not retaining the dream. Go to the movies, support your friends' dreams, and celebrate other people's successes. Don't be a dick – be a friend.

The movie experience is a wonderful feeling. It is a place to get lost and forget about your problems. If you can't see the connection between the movies and me, then go back to page one and re-read my story.

Ke Huy Quan - Data from THE GOONIES won an Academy Award later in his life because he never gave up on his dream.

So many of my 1980's film stars have passed on but have never left my heart. I still see them in all their glory up there on the screen. I still hear the lines and all the quotes.

Remember that Goonies never say die!

When your Ego

# CHAPTER TEN

## *MY CHILDREN*

*"Parenting without a sense of humor is like being an accountant who sucks at math."—*
*Amber Dusick*

Since I am a closed off and unemotional, never giving praise type of asshole, this chapter is intended to tell my kids the words I rarely do. I LOVE YOU. They have grown used to my inability to climb out from within my own internal strife. They've called me out numerous times but never left me behind, and they may occasionally ask me if I do indeed love them, but they usually

When your Ego

just enjoy my discomfort while trying to answer the question. This may go poorly because even though I have worked hard to get here, the devil side still says, "toughen the fuck up. These kids aren't here to be your friend. You love them with actions – no one needs the words."

This is the go-to reply when you are an asshole.

I have mentioned my children and all the importance they played in my survival. The comedic truth lies in who they have become. Those miserable little shit heads have managed to make me proud. They are far from perfect. In fact, their flaws spread everywhere, and often somehow still become my problem.

One of them is far more responsible than the other but that isn't any different than most siblings. I won't mention names or who is my assumed favorite. (Yes, parents have favorites.) I won't say that my daughter receives more direct love from me than the others. And I won't reveal their flaws.

All the previous statements are outright lies. Anyone who knows me knows that Riley is the most local, the most active in checking in, and thus receives the most adoration. This shouldn't surprise the other kids; they are aware, and it is often mentioned in texts. But this chapter isn't intended to cause more division. I prefer that things remain civil. I don't mind a little conflict when it's kept within the confines of our privacy but sharing with the entire world to read, may increase the likelihood that I have mysteriously taken ill.

The point is – MY CHILDREN ARE OUT TO KILL ME.

I feel that they have a secret text chain between them meticulously planning my demise. Sometimes they ask me questions that tell my gut that they have a perfect plan. This isn't a new feeling. All kids slowly murder us with every painstaking moment since sliding out of the vag. Maybe shortening vagina for shock value is considered cheap, but I really enjoy a fun word choice for anatomy.

When your Ego

Now that I've deflected as usual, let's get on with my intended sentiment. I suppose procrastinating and delaying will NOT deliver the proposed message. My kids have never read anything I have written, so this is mostly a filler. See how fucked up my go to of humor overrides any accolades? Is it impossible for me to just say I love you? Unfortunately, it is a haunting repetitive problem that I have dealt with for years.

**ANTHONY**

I will begin this with my son Anthony. He was born March 6th, 1993, in the middle of a late Winter storm. I was nervous but hid it well. I remember thinking how my driving mattered greatly. I knew he was a boy, and I was ready to meet my kid. My mother was the nurse on duty, so that was a bonus to his birth.

Anthony arrived – healthy and amazing. I watched through the nursery window as my mother doted over him sweetly. Having a blood related nurse inoculate and bathe is a gift that most parents and children rarely receive. I was elated to prove that I could be someone's father.

Let's cut through the bullshit. I had no business having children. I had no money or future. My marriage was a complete sham, and we were living with my in- laws. The responsibility level used in these decisions was built on my own selfishness and needs. But I absolutely loved this baby. He changed the way I thought about myself, which in turn motivated me to become better.

Did it work? Not exactly.

I did possess the natural abilities to be a caring father. I'd like to think that growing up being the only boy surrounded by women transferred a few of their feminine instincts. That's just my own personal assumption without any scientific data to back it up. I still believe, even if it isn't the truth, that the females in my life played a role.

Anthony was an easy baby. I stress "baby" because the older years excelled the problems. His energy level was always an issue. This kid

When your Ego bounced off walls like rubber balls dropped from the sky. He had an intense desire to be injured from a fall.

## **MY CONTINUED GUILT**

At three years old, Anthony decided to hang out with his old man while I cleaned up the yard. Substantial water damage had forced my father-in-law to restructure a portion of the home's foundation. The only way I could feel like half an actual man, rather than a sub-standard piece of shit – was to pull my weight by doing manual labor as a rent payment.

So here I am, taking broken pieces of concrete blocks and tossing them into the woods. Anthony was being his typical self and roaming throughout the yard. When he walked into the path of my concrete flight, I quickly caught it and asked him not to get in the path. He listened well and made his way to the other end of the yard.

Moments later and without my awareness, he made his way behind me. As I went into my backswing with the concrete block. It caught him beneath the chin with full force. His teeth protruded through the bottom of his lip and the blood poured from his mouth like a waterfall. I swooped him into my arms and ran towards my car.

I was shirtless and holding him on my chest as I drove. No seatbelt and at an incredible excessive speed. The first doctor turned us away due to lack of medical insurance, so we quickly drove to the hospital.

My panic and anxiety levelled. They took him to the back and gave me a wet towel to clean the blood from my skin. After providing me with a purple shirt to cover myself up, they took me into the back where I had hoped to sit beside my son.

They sat me in a private office when two men entered. They introduced themselves as law enforcement for the state and needed to ask a few questions. I obliged and asked about the wellbeing of my child.

When your Ego

"It's not good sir, can you explain to us what happened?"

I told my version of the story and then again three hours later. In the fifth hour it began a good cop bad cop scenario.

One would say, "just tell us you hit him with intent, and we can let you see him."

The other pretended to be my friend. His words more softly spoken, "We understand, we have kids and understand the pressures of discipline. If you hit him just tell us. It will all be okay and then you can see him."

I nearly cracked and admitted guilt just so I could see him. After eight hours, I was released when Anthony's story matched mine.

They managed to stitch him up and the damage was limited to baby teeth and a cut.

I still feel so much guilt from that day. Anthony is fine today and has no memory of this accident. His teeth grew back, and I hope he is taking loving care of them.

## ANTHONY THE STUDENT

This part is left brief because Anthony the student doesn't exist. Take time to reflect on the important stuff.

## ANTHONY THE ATHLETE

But Anthony the student athlete does exist. He was phenomenal and this is where I can speak. His cheerleading level reached the highest levels and I secretly indulged in the attention as the father of the best.

Often, I would walk into an event and see the people begin to whisper, "that's his dad." And often pointing. This made me feel so good inside. I know it's selfish, but I really did support his talent. When he flipped, I flipped. When he

When your Ego was injured, I was injured. We suffered and celebrated together. It's all metaphorical but it's how I felt at the moments.

Now I know what you are thinking – only gay boys would be cheerleaders. It's not true at all. There are numerous "straight" male cheerleaders cheering all over the world. But, to let the cat from the bag – Anthony is gay. OMG, shocker – I knew it. Yes, he is a happy, successful, and a married gay man – and no matter how you think on the subject, I am over the moon supportive and proud.

And if you are a hateful or just a piece of shit who thinks gay means wrong, then go fuck yourself.

The world has enough hatred in it. I understand you not understanding, but to hate blindly based on it is atrocious and a notable example of you being a piece of shit.

To end my words on child one, let me try and be as open and honest as possible. Anthony once called me (drunk) at three in the morning. He asked me if I loved him. I answered him through my foggy sleepy voice. The answer was yes.

Yes, since the minute I saw you. Yes, through all the struggles. It has always been yes. You helped me by challenging my thinking every day of your life. Whether it was your antics or telling me your orientation. I love everything – redact that – I love most everything you are.

None of my love will ever waver. I will do my best to continue my support. Whether it's your piano playing or your gay right fights. Daddy has your back.

## **RILEY**

Let's get into this little bossy, mouthy, overprotective hellcat. Born September 12, 2000, in between a Red Sox doubleheader. The Sox won.

Riley was a tougher birth than her brother. The shear size of her watermelon head alone would scare other women from vaginal births. I got to see it firsthand as my mother once again

When your Ego

was the nurse on duty and the doctors allowed me to catch the exit.

It was a perfect mix of beauty and gross. The goo and slime involved is overwhelming. The experience was worth the mess. I was elated to be the first hands to hold her, and I haven't let go of her since.

Her early life was unfortunately a mess. I had left and filed for divorce prior to her second birthday. The truth is she was a fix it baby. An unplanned ploy to try and repair our family. It didn't work and rarely does. Nonetheless, I am happy she arrived.

I missed a lot because of numerous issues. One being the main income source for multiple households. Two having to work several jobs and three because I was now a single man. None of them are good enough excuses but it's the truth. I put my new and exciting single life in front of my kids, and I regret it.

Riley went on to follow in her brothers' footsteps. Although, she didn't exceed her brother's skill level, she did teach me something that every parent should hear. When the second child follows the supreme athlete, we need to recognize that challenge. Riley wasn't referred to as Riley Carroll, instead she became the sister of Anthony. It put unwanted pressures that disallowed her to shine on her own. Whenever we judge someone based on another example, we lessen their abilities.

She also became a great student athlete despite the challenge. She completed high school as a better student than her brother, and all before turning eighteen. I, myself never exceeded the ninth grade. If the goal was to have my children be better than me, then I won. Although I never set the bar exceedingly high, both kids probably passed it in the fifth grade.

Riley has been my constant nag. The parent to the parent and the one girl who has no trouble calling me out on my bullshit. She has maturity beyond her years yet loves me in ways no one else ever could. Beyond her beauty, no thanks to me, she is fun, funny, moody and an amazing friend. Her hair stylist talents are through the roof, and her attitude is proportionate to that minute. (Beware of the moods.)

The genuine concern she showed in the loss of her mother was an achievement that she met head on. I have never felt more pride. No twenty-one-year-old should have to do what she did. If there's a message in this, be sure to get your end of life in order. No one wants to think of their demise, but I'm here to tell you that one day you will die.

Her openness is alarming to most. She and I discuss everything. It could be relationships, birth control, her boyfriend's actions, or life in general. We have very few secrets and I suppose this is a good thing, considering this book is filled with a few of mine.

This child truly saved my life. She added and instilled in me the bravery to face my demons head on. She allows me to be myself, even when I am a fool. I don't have any excuse to not say I love you. So, right here, in this fucking book – I will shout it out for all to hear, I love you baby girl.

**On a sidenote** – she also allows me to still track her whereabouts. And I take full advantage of it.

## ALYSSA MY MISSING CHILD

I saved this for the end of the chapter. Not because of rank or order, but because I am so afraid of putting my feelings into words. I don't want to lose myself, but I fear that not losing it will not resolve the issue. Truthfully, it just may be too late to save our relation.

She was born on May 19th, and I was not invited. I didn't even know until her mother surprised me in my job parking lot about two weeks later. She rolled down her window and asked, "Do you want to meet your daughter?" I responded, regrettably, "That's not my kid."

I walked away and to my car.

Yes, I was nineteen and broke. I truly had no guarantee the child was mine, but in hindsight I

When your Ego

didn't need to comment so rudely. In writing, right here, I apologize to her mother.

The next two years involved court cases and blood tests. I did all that I could to make sure I was the father. The test came back as a 99.9 percent match, and I was a father – sort of. I say sort of because at the time men didn't have much power or respect in these situations. I never earned any rights either and that's on me.

So now I have a child with zero visitation rights. I was ordered to pay, I believe $115.00 weekly, directly from my paycheck. Eventually, coincidentally because of my wife pulling strings behind my back, I began to see her on weekends. She was seven.

How the fuck can anyone form any bond with a seven-year-old. She was timid and shy. This is an example of both parents just trying to damage the other. An immature result of having children so young. Unfortunately, my mother paid the debt and had nothing to do with my mistakes. It hurt her deeply to not be as involved as she wanted. Between her sickness and the drama, it took precious time away.

After all the difficulties – mostly on my end, Alyssa did turn eighteen and started to visit on her own. All was fine, we had limited bond, but I loved her and wanted her to succeed. Then things went south. I never understood where all the bitterness was coming from but as I aged, I understood. This kid did nothing wrong. She never asked to be born and only wanted to be loved. I didn't provide it in my limited role, and the bad labeling by the others in her life could have helped in her decisions.

When my mother passed, I was dealing with the loss. A phone call from her set me off and I reacted not wrongly, but without thought of consequence. She said, "I am sorry that your mom died. I didn't know her." – that's not verbatim but the basics of what was said. I reacted poorly. Cancelled her schooling I was providing and the phone for which I was paying. All reactions I wish I never did.

I took such offense to the added condolence.

When your Ego

That's when the visits and phone calls ended. She married and left her sister and me off the guest list. The wedding was a mile from my home, but I was not included – rightfully so. I never earned that gift. She had a stepfather she called dad. I was nothing more than a desperate man with an open wallet trying to buy her forgiveness.

All of this is tragic. All of this, or most, is on me. She never knew me or wanted to, and her mother didn't know me at all. I was cast aside as the sperm donor and lived with that thought process for many years.

I used to reach out to her on holidays and her birthdays. I stopped once I realized my holidays or birthdays didn't matter. She genuinely wants nothing to do with me or her siblings. And this is all because of a one-night stand where two children made a choice.

Because I am not able to have any contact with her child (my grandchild) – I feel like a piece of shit. I once stood in line behind my granddaughter at a Walmart in my town, and all I could do was be silent. It was fucking heartbreaking.

So now we are caught up. We have zero connection or contact. I don't know what else I could do this late in our lives. But I am alive and a decent man. I am no longer the man I was and was never the man she was taught through her mother. I paid my court ordered support and made attempts to reconcile. This is the most devastating feeling in my life. It feels so defeating to waste the opportunities.

So, to Alyssa, I am here, and I love you. I cannot repair the past, but I can show you who I've become. I have no legitimate excuse beyond being young and having not yet dealt with my personal trauma. None of that is on you, I know this. But I am alive and well, but we are not promised to be here tomorrow. We have time today. We can heal the issues and I will do my best to be a part of a solution.

When your Ego

# CHAPTER ELEVEN

## *FUTURE PLANS*

*"The future belongs to those who believe in the beauty of their dreams." -- Eleanor Roosevelt*

What a great positive quote from a lovely voice, but if you've been paying attention, my core thinking doesn't exactly exude positivity. Sure, I can speak it and portray the urgency of being a positive speaker, but do I live it in my daily life? Not always.

I am a perpetual pessimist with the desire to become a shiny positive person. Unfortunately, this will never happen. I am not upset about it and love the fact that I often will take the negative side of the debate. I like to ask problematic questions and take the devils advocate side of an argument.

I still always strive to do my best. Whether it's life, work, my podcasts, or my books. I really do

When your Ego

explore different avenues between my likes and dislikes. I tend to remain a far too open book when discussing things that others consider as private. Obviously, if you've read this far, I rarely find it difficult to talk. Even if the subject is considered taboo – I am on it.

    Let's explore those platforms I utilize and try to find an explanation for my madness.

## **LIFE**

    Up until the last five years or so, I always had to be the one who spoke up whenever a debate began. I usually used common sense with a dash of intelligence to argue with whoever was speaking. I may have even internally agreed with them but couldn't help trying to antagonize them with some opposition.

    Its part being an asshole but more a way to increase the chances of me giving two shits what you believe to be an interesting point.

    I highly despise a few subjects and when these are brought up in a talking point, my mind instantly thinks of ways to fuck it up. It's a horrible way to live but a lot of fucking fun.

    I enjoy the way the eyes of others begin to dilate. They usually know I am going to do this yet still insist on involving me in their debate. To me, that's on them. If you know my reaction, then deal with its consequence.

    Politics is an easy discussion for me. I have many friends who support each party involved but I could sit on my asshole fence and twist to either side. I used to enjoy it until Trump entered the fray. And I am less anti Trump than the previous sentence presents. Unfortunately, he created a new breed of debaters, and they love to get angry if you question them with intelligence.

    The truth I am here to divulge is that I never have and never will care about national politics. They are all dick bags with too much power. It's the least fun active arguments I could be involved with.

When your Ego

One – it's easy to play on both sides of the fence. Two – I somehow figured a way to piss off both sides in one paragraph.

Example:

"I think all illegal aliens should have to leave unless they are gay."

"I believe they should ban all guns and abortions."

By agreeing and disagreeing at the same time, it really ignites the masses. Nothing fucks with the human mind like an intelligent asshole.
Now I no longer join in. People have become so invested in one belief or another, that they are now willing to fight or end a friendship in a political disagreement. It's ridiculous. The only time I activate my asshole ways is when someone says something so vehemently stupid that I need to let others know. It's not an exceptional quality but it sure is a lot of fun.

The next argument I stopped getting in is over sports. Particularly when it's a debate over who is better. It's such a useless argument and rarely are you able to sway your opponent from their opinions.

The problem is that whenever you are talking about a player or team you are a fan of your fandom rarely will allow you to switch. It's a debate about favoritism that solves no issues and makes little movement in the world.

No one cares about your opinion – even if they say they do. Your Facebook or social media post is NOT moving the needle at all. You are a plumber with three ex wives and five children you never see – let's tone down the agenda and go raise your fucking kids.

## **THE PODCAST**

My comedy is not for all. And I know not everything I find funny will correlate to the majority. I am fine with all of this. Usually

When your Ego

everything heard on my shows is thought up on the fly. I don't hit homeruns every time. Some would argue that I swing and miss more than others. My advice is always the same – TURN IT OFF. I do want people to listen, but I shouldn't have to submiss my thinking to satisfy yours. There are millions of other shows and thousands that fit your agendas. I will include the link for eBook formats and the name for other formats to search.

**A DUDE IN THE HENHOUSE –**
**Is available wherever you listen to Podcasts or on YOUTUBE**

On the shows I guest spot or host, my argumentative style is more accepted. The whole point of a discussion is to give all the facts known from both points of view. It is a form of acting and I do a decent job at entertaining my listeners.

Recently, we ran into a minor issue of complaints due to my cohost Mel remarking on how men feel in a certain sexual situation. I feel that if I had asked the question then none of this would have been mentioned as a concern.

Women should have the same open forum to discuss sexuality. We all do it and nothing Mel said was out of line or not discussed between women on private chats. The point of our show is to discuss the opinions between men and women. It's educational, fun, and informative. It's time for people to learn how to turn the channel rather than jump onto social media to complain.

If you would like to be a guest – send us a message.

## **WORK**

Although I wrote a lot of this prior, this specific work issue arose, and I wanted it included. It's a good example of how my personal change works against me at times.

I was fired, terminated, asked to exit, cancelled and embarrassed for providing water and drinks for the humans who I supervised.

Working overnights during a hot July in a brick oven building without A/C, my understaffed

When your Ego

and overworked employees gave everything that they humanly could.  The vending machines were broken on one night, not accepting cash on another, and out of stock the next. As their supervisor, I offered cold drinks – took their orders from them and provided hydration where no other options were available.

    The process intended when a supervisor does this is to remember to charge them off six hours later when the store opens. I did not complete this process and was charged with theft. The total cost of loss was $18.55, to which I offered to pay immediately.

    Without mentioning the well-known employer who sells hardware across the USA, I was suspended pending an investigation. Upon leaving I inquired about the period and was told that in 2-5 days I would be contacted.

    No contact ever arrived. I discovered my termination ten days later when my dentist couldn't put my insurance through their system. Turns out, they terminated me 2 days into the suspension.

My reason for telling this ridiculous story is to point out what I believe cost me my job. My newfound desire to care for humans may have played a role.

A few weeks prior to this dismissal, I was having issues with one of my employees. His mental health and home life were causing a lack of work ethic and availability. I went to my superiors as I had been invited to deal with these problems. We discussed my concerns and the employees' reasons.

The advice given by both Derek and Jimmy was to work him harder and force him to quit.

Because I had a newfound compassion for anyone suffering, I declined this option. One, because it's not humane and two, for my safety. I did not want to be the heavy that cost this mans ability to feed his family. I did not want to cause more harm to his mental health.

I should mention that this corporate identity advertised vehemently about their concerns for mental health. After investigating it further, it was

When your Ego

no more than a mediocre at best program designed to make it impossible to qualify.

From that day forward my work life changed. They mentioned to me that I may not have the needed supervisory skills to remain as one in their employment.

If I had remained the previous version of myself, none of this would have happened. I would have gladly pushed my crew beyond their limits to selfishly prosper on the back end. I didn't care about how people felt. If you came to work, you worked. I didn't have time for your home issues or inside mentality.

I feel as if I did exactly what a supervisor is meant to do. I took care of the wellbeing of my workers to keep them safe and hydrated. Losing my job based on my actions hurts my pride and my ego. It didn't kill my concerns for those humans.

As I write this part, I have not received any form of income in 6 weeks. But, if I could change the corporate mindset on mental health and wellness, I would gladly become homeless in its efforts. My workers are people not machines. Even machines receive maintenance and care. I won't say who I worked for, but I will tell you that this hardware store's colors were NOT orange. I won't mention last names with the masterminds of retail who didn't show concern for their workers, but they go by Derek – Casey and Jimmy.

These are three men who profit from the workers. Three men who have sold their souls to the corporate way and dismissed any external concerns toward others. I am bitter and disgusted because I poured myself into being the best supervisor possible. They understaffed purposely to profit. They overworked purposely to cash in. I witnessed numerous unrepaired violations and have proof if needed of payroll skimming.

I won't reveal my pictures or proof and will allow karma alone to change their futures – and it will. My intent isn't revenge but writing a memoir gives me some creative liberties and this replicates some of the reasons I have

When your Ego changed for the better. Sometimes being a better person will not move you up the work ladder. Remain true to yourself and prosper honestly with your dignity still intact.

**<u>FINAL NOTES:</u>**

We just need to be kinder. We need to find some compassion. It's detrimental to your health and mental stability. Being negative and hateful against anything you disagree with will eat you alive. Niceness isn't emasculating - Aggression isn't strength. It's quite the opposite.

When your Ego

# CHAPTER TWELVE

## *UNINTENDED REWARDS*

"Anything less than the truth is paralysis."

It's a beautifully said quote, but not mine. I heard it while listening to Howard Stern in an interview with John Stamos. He, like me, dealt with similar young life trauma. Of course, my success could never match his, but that's the point of me writing this book.

I have somehow learned through time passed and other experiences, that our successes aren't measured equally. Some compare notoriety, some prefer cashflow. Some base it from fame but I choose to mark it with my next morning. It's less flashy and a lot more difficult to pay my bills with, but it's honest. I celebrate waking up and loving my life.

I have managed to Shawshank this trauma. I crawled through a lifetime of shit and came out clean on the other side. Like Andy Dufresne, I needed to go away and hide for a while. In the end, my good friend returned. I manifested my life into a positive.

When I began this book and decided where it should begin, I chose a recent break up. I revealed how I viewed the situation in the moment. That was ten years ago and today I am happily involved with my perfect match. I am not saying that my next nonfiction book won't begin with her leaving me, but the point is time changes most things for the better. Usually, I am always a skeptic. I analyze and research and deduct an answer that isn't always correct. I have lived through so much and in every case, the future result was worth the pain.

When your Ego

So, since I love to analyze things into oblivion. Let's explore the cause and results of the previous chapters.

1. **FAILED RELATIONSHIPS**

In the first one as mentioned above - that man no longer exists. He's a ghost. I needed to be used and manipulated. I am not half of who I am without that woman who I had thought was my future. We were merely ships on different oceans and slowly sinking. What she added to me, I hope I did the same. I was not innocent in its demise.

She is the first person who I allowed to hurt me, that I completely detached away from. It feels great. I saw that her negatives outweighed her good, and I stepped away. That became a waterfall effect. I became aggressive in my rebuilding and eliminated the waste in my life. If you can cut the fat from your life, you will succeed in finding peace.

The pieces of her that I enjoyed are missed, but not forgotten. Her version of the story may differ from mine. When one person is willing to seek mental health assistance and the other hasn't yet hit bottom, this is the result every time. You alone cannot save another person if you don't first save yourself.

I use that relationship as an example of what I no longer ever want. If my current relation is faltering, there's conversation and dialogue, respect, and resolve. It really is that easy if you put in one hundred percent.

### 2. **MUSIC AS A CURE**

Chapter two spoke about allowing music to affect your misery. Although this remains true, I have learned how to control how the music moves me. Music is never a bad choice. The power it holds is far less dangerous than a bottle of liquor or pills. Lyrics and rhythm soothe much more than hurt. The emotions it causes are strengthening moments that become tools. The tools then help to rebuild. It's a process of failure as a lesson, then the lesson as the future result.

I suffered. I felt the weight breaking me and music was never the culprit.

As I said in that chapter, the songs will never do anything but heal. People with dementia hear a song and instantly remember the words. They can't recall a loved one or the day of the week, but they remember the music.

3. **SEXUAL MOLESTATION**

In Chapter three we explored my sexual molestation and its impact on my future. This was the toughest and least in-depth written part. Why did I not write it as deep? The answer sadly is that the reminder of the time hurt me greatly. I spent hours suffering from recall and it only took a few hours of writing before the past returned to haunt me.

I felt so useless in these writing moments. An author handcuffed and chained to his past as it presented itself once again. I could feel her hands, hear her voice – it all returned as a giant storm cloud pouring down upon me, collapsing on my soul, and crushing me where I sat.

One of the hardest parts about this book is the anxiety it created. Not only by the stories but also by the critics once it's released. I procrastinated while focusing on the future impact rather than the writing. I knew the intention was to help others in similar circumstances, but I never could shake the guilt of lowering my masculinity. All – ironically, my Ego.

I found the comedy more difficult to utilize. I wanted to deflect as usual but couldn't find the funny. I wanted and needed to tell this story but never expected the trauma returning. I am good now, but it took me a few weeks to continue.

I do believe I am better now than ever. The truth has been released and I feel relieved.

### 4. DIVORCE

Chapter four moved into my upbring and parents' divorce – I was able to open a more honest dialogue within my family. I had questions never asked. Now I simply ask. I take my shot. It's been met with a lot of mixed responses. Mostly due to the years between removing the memory.

I never understood as a young boy, that whenever I asked my dad a question involving a date, he would stumble. I used to think, "how could he not know when this happened?" Now I understand. It happens as we age, and the years begin to multiply.

### 5. MY MARRIAGE

Chapter five went into my marriage and my ex-wife's demise. This chapter taught me a lot about responsibility and compassion. I am proud of the way I wrote it. It's a far cry to what I could have written ten years prior. I didn't allow the past to sway my thoughts. I explored the situation maturely and was able to leave a historical recollection of her life.

It's so important to allow the past to breathe. If I hadn't that chapter would have included a whole lot of fucks and anger. Without my ex I don't have those kids to drive me fucking nutty. I don't have the lessons that taught me how to overcome adversity and be a better man for the next person.

I hope I remained fair and haven't let my children down.

## 6. <u>RELIGION</u>

Next, I decided that religion needed to be discussed. A dangerous conversation in my family but a needed one for me. Even after all this reflection on my life, I do NOT believe a higher power is present. I am unsure if I ever will.

Being a skeptic and atheist has its drawbacks. How nice it must feel to think there is more when we pass. I recognize so many amazing people in this world, that at times it's harder to not believe. I also see the beauty – the mountains, the ocean, the animals, the flowers. I am paying attention, but I unfortunately see all the dreadful things.

I will never understand why so many people die in the name of religious indifference. Why

When your Ego

are children starving and others lost on a path of drugs and addiction. Why are the homeless left behind? I see so much tragedy and can not think about the goodness of your God.

The scientific side tends to impress me most. I can say that I hope I am wrong. People who know me also know the role that the great writer Stephen King plays in my life. Whenever he is doing a tour, you can find me there. I find his ability to weave words into stories fascinating. Even his books considering as less leave a part of their characters in my head. Think of how Taylor Swift fans react to her. Well, I am "A Stevey."

During a meet and greet at the amazing MARK TWAIN HOUSE, I got to hob knob with my writing hero like a true stalker. It was relaxed and just a bunch of similarly obsessed fans hoping to get a hello. During the question portion, someone asked how he deals with being considered demonic, then followed with his religious beliefs.

Stephen mentions the same passage in his book, ON WRITING.

"I chose to believe in God because it makes things better. You have a meditation point, a source of strength". He continued,

" I choose to believe that God exists, and therefore I can say, God, I can't do this by myself. Help me not to take a drink today. Help me not to take a drug today. And that works fine for me."

This is a well thought out decision and respected by me. I understand his points and how that helps him continue his recovery. I use this story as a reference to make your own choices. Just because my hero believes doesn't mean I must. And if we can mutually respect and discuss our debate like two humans who are sensible, then maybe the world can become better.

### 7-8. SUICIDE EFFECT

Suicide rates have climbed every year of my life. The facts and the stats show no relief in

When your Ego

sight. The grief of the world suffers the same. This is no longer an American problem, it's a worldwide epidemic. I have a deep and concerned passion for the problem and I think together as humans we can lower the impact.

Statistically, I am a piece of the existing problem. I tried the best I could to explain my ideations, but I also feel guilty of making excuses. How could I be a part of the solution, yet a part of the problem?

I guess it's time to divulge that today, in 2023, I am no longer suffering similarly and have no ideations left inside. I struggle like everyone else but have found alternative solutions to the problems. The most important is the woman who stands beside me. She isn't a cure, she isn't without flaws, but she cares. She holds me responsible and loves me for all my flaws.

It seems simplistic and unrealistic that one single human could sway my life and outlook – but it is true. I could honestly say that because of the late start in age, and the beginning of the relation, has me wanting to live forever. I deserve her and she inspires my future.

So, if one single human could sway me, why can't a bunch of compassionate humans save the world? Maybe if we all gather and begin to understand suicide as a health issue, then maybe we could be a part of the solution. Even if you can't directly focus on solving it, you could start by being kind. Kindness kills the demons. It is a powerful skill and easily accomplished. Kindness isn't learned, it is in us all.

The sign off to all my podcasts is "if no one has told you they love you today, I (we) love you"

I say it every week on (shameless plug) A DUDE IN THE HENHOUSE & HAPPY HOUR with SCOTT H. SILVERMAN.

I love to say it and I mean it. The world is such a fucked-up place, and too many people go all day without any support. Just try for a week to help someone else. I promise the karma will come back to you in one way or another. A new quote I heard that fits came from the great Travis Kelce on his podcast NEW HEIGHTS.

"You are either a fountain or a drain – be a fountain."

## 9. DREAMS

I needed to write this chapter. I may not have said all I needed to, but I value the price of not chasing dreams. I lived it, I still do. I continue to be a procrastinating fool who is waiting for permission to succeed. What a fucking moronic mindset.

Without dreams and aspirations, you are limited in your future. I don't quite buy into the "if you have a plan B, you have no dream." But I do subscribe to never giving up on the process.

Without a dream, what is the juice that flows through you?

Without the dream where does your energy grow?

Dreams are necessary to survive. And not everyone's dream needs to involve fame. As a writer, I encourage others to author their story. With the tools available today, everyone has the skill. Everything else is hirable and easily found.

YouTube provides millions of how to videos from many accredited institutions.

Now, before you sit down and chase that dream, relax. You are not an author. I speak on this a lot because it bugs the shit out of me. Amazon may have simplified the process of becoming a published writer, but without the hours of experience, you are not yet granted the claim of author. I will dive a bit deeper but if this isn't your thing, just move forward. I promise not to bore the fuck out of you with my opinions.

The invention of the indie Published books has blessed us with opportunities that unfortunately has been squandered. It's been so watered down by "writers" who have been told that they've written a masterpiece.

Relax, you haven't.

The cause and effects have hurt the legitimate writer who publishes his or her work. The scenario I have seen since I released my first novella, is this.

When your Ego

I imagine the buyer spending their hard-earned cash to buy the book that others are sharing. It has a great sexy cover with some half naked heartthrob sprawled out. The typography is correct. And then like a gut punch to the belly fat – the story goes fucking nowhere.

Now, the purchaser is gun shy on their next purchase.

I am NOT a huge fan of sex in books. As a man, we do not have the emotional value to properly type a sexual situation without it appearing as a rape scene. I know this is personal and shocking to my friends who have successfully made it in erotic writing.

Without calling them out and lessening their abilities, I do not mean it doesn't deserve a place. Many men exist with the ability. NICOLAS SPARKS, comes to mind, but my gripe is not on his level. Here is my useless theory.

The quote, "Don't judge a book by its cover," is not a great quote for books. It refers more to the human than a physical marketing plan. It is quite the opposite in self-publishing. Many writers have discovered that the cover is the sale. Amazon only gives you about three inches of visibility and if that sight illuminates the buyer, then the story doesn't matter.

I subscribe to the theory that a bad book with a great cover always outsells a great one with a shit cover. I will go down fighting this theory. Hence why the romance erotica genre seems to never die. I have several friends who make a decent living off this smut. So, obviously I am in the minority. My Facebook is flooded with images of muscular men scantily dressed and strutting their stuff. I hate it all.

How many ways can you fuck?

Apparently, enough to satisfy the readers.

My point is that whatever genre you choose – create a quality story. I would much rather profit from my story being enjoyed than my cover model. Maybe I am wrong, if so, I don't apologize.

When your Ego

I do NOT mean to disregard your cover. The marketing relies on it because it is all you have currently to show. I do it. I love the process and now I am contradicting myself once again. The steps to becoming a thriving author require a completed process. The story comes first – then the edit – then the layout – then the fucking cover. Do your best, put in the time and efforts, then pray someone who is not a friend or relative fucking cares. Push sharing and be relentless in your tasks. All the rest is out of your hands.

And don't get me started on bestselling lists. Too late – here I go. I am divulging too much back behind the scenes information, but guess who garners the reward of obtaining a book on the list? Yep, you guessed it – whoever pays for it the most. This is not everyone, some are worthy, but the majority is a purchased award.

Being an author is an honor. Some, judging by the comments under my books may disagree with me referring to myself as one. But I have put in the time. I failed, I've succeeded, and I have spent many lonely nights writing when my friends are all out having sex. Go author your story. If it sells that's amazing. If it doesn't, remember the dream – keep fucking writing.

## 10. MY CHILDREN

This whole book and my life do not exist without them. I am a fake tough prick who has a sad sap loving father trapped inside. I need to begin allowing him out. My children deserve it, and it is so much easier on your soul.

I am not going to wax poetic about how amazing my kids are because that's not how I speak. I make them aware of their successes and failures. I rarely compare them, and I sadly never tell them I love them.

The I love you part is the worst flaw I carry. It has never come easily but I am getting better. The bullshit excuse would be from not feeling loved as a child, but that's a complete cop out. I could tell the world about all my pains and defeats but somehow, I can't just tell them I love you.

It's time to call myself out and take responsibility. Whether it's ten or a million copies sold, all of you who read this now know my promise. Here it is in print. I will start and let down my deflector. I will let my kids know that I love them. They know it in actions, but they deserve to also hear it.

## 11. **FUTURE PLANS**

Plans are a nice thought but rarely pan out. I am going to focus on today and try not to worry about tomorrow. I will continue to write, and I will eventually provide the stories I chose not to tell in this release.

When your Ego

# LUCKY THIRTEEN

### LET'S NOT SAY GOODBYE – LET'S JUST SAY FAREWELL

*"I wish you all a long and happy life."*

It is October 27, 2023, coincidentally the birthday of two of my three sisters. I was sure to talk with them both and the reason I am telling you is that is part of the changes I made. My family stuff matters. I recognize the differences, the past and the pain caused, but you can't switch who or the family to which you are born.

You could hide away and live your time a miserable lonely fellow, or you can forgive.

    I still wouldn't change a thing about my life. The terrible things that happened and the poor choices I made have all brought me here. This is far from the end of my story, but I plan for the rest to be glorious.

    My life choices created better options for my recovery and now I sit here still bruised by the past but sufficiently rebuilt and running at full steam. I am merely bruised. I will heal because I set goals and put a focus on being better. I will never be perfect and will remain flawed. Parts of the old me exist and will never die but I will continue to do my best.

    The stories I told are the best recollected versions of my memories. I tried to be as transparent with them as possible but other underlying issues relegated a few of the stories to cliff notes. Some laws exist to protect the guilty and once those run their course, I will write a second book.

When your Ego

The most important parts to me are that my stories impact and effect it has on you the reader helps. I have mentioned how my trauma doesn't compare to others, and yours won't compare to theirs. The sooner we realize that all trauma matters, the sooner we all can find our way.

Everything that happens in our lives has an alternate way to escape it. My discussion of suicide ideation was just an older version of me and not an answer to any problems. I have watched not only my friends succeed at the act, but also too many parents suffer with the loss of a child. It is NOT the way to escape. The pain that it leaves behind for others to manage only creates a transfer of depression. A vicious circle of misery. I believe that Therapy and telling your story can assist, but it takes your strength and willpower to return from the darkness. It's worth the effort and I would like to help.

In the back of the book, I will include links and information that can help. I can never guarantee it absolves you from your problems, but it is a beginning to understand something clearly at last.

    I wish I had a witty remark or a way to save the world. I wish I had cared more at a younger age, and I could have listened and helped. I am here now and plan to be for a while.
    I have visited the darkest ends of the night and suffered with thoughts to end my life. I assumed wrongly that no one cared and that no one else could understand. Assumptions will not move you forward. I found strength in the simple joy of wonder. The world may be a fucked-up place – filled with fucked up issues, but they are repairable.
    You matter. You matter to someone, you matter to strangers, you matter to me. The world may not see you today but tomorrow has a whole new beginning. Without sounding like a preacher, let me tell you that the fight is a rough road to remain stable on. It's filled with unpaved paths with ruts and obstacles. The twists and turns come on sudden and it is much easier to wander from the road and give up.

When your Ego

We aren't here to quit. You have all the fucking power and strength to conquer this road. Yes, it's going to trip you up and perhaps you will fall – but if you get back up, that's a win. If you stay down, you won't. keep fighting. Keep moving. One day becomes two then weeks become a month. In no time at all the years pass by and you grow.

Once you commit to healing your past distances itself in your rearview mirror. If I can rebound and repair it, there is no doubt that you can too.

Obviously, I like to joke around – that's my personality deflecting my hurt. It is potentially helpful if you find something that works for you. let your personality replace the alcohol or drugs being abused to temporarily numb your existence.

And I understand why you use it because I did it. I saw cocaine and alcohol as my shutoff switch. The only problem is all I did was swap one problem for another. Eventually this addiction becomes friends with your misery, and they work together to kill you off.

You don't owe anyone a show. Go execute your happiness and spend time with the people who support your dreams.

And remember that girl who I somehow fell for forty years ago? Well, the universe has placed her right beside me. We have evolved and are now involved. A notable example of patience and earning what you covet. I realize that it may not be forever, but for now, we are willing to make things work. Yay, me.

Before I end this book – try to remember some of my words. If you wander from the path, just find your way back. I promise you the world is a gift.

I realize that I won't last forever. I have come to an agreement with myself on this subject and accept it for what it is. We all must end, but it doesn't mean today. I have a well-planned out demise that's a far way off that I would like to share.

## When your Ego

If you have read this far, you know religious belief is not in this head. I may be wrong and if I am, I hope I get a second chance. But I want my second chance with the people I failed. I want to live my childhood with the understanding of what my parents may have gone through with their own personal traumas. I want to try this all again. Just give me a chance to re-live it.

I'd like to see that one special girl sitting beside me as I draw my final breath. I want her to be unaffected by my passing and proud of the man I've become. I want the final movie that flashes through my head to be of my children laughing at my jokes with all my friends smiling. And I want the final scene to be the girls from 1987 shaking their asses on the McDonald's tabletop.

And if all of that is not possible – please give me the one girl I managed to love for most of my life – and just give me one final kiss.

Thank you for reading my book.

# - THE END

When your Ego

# CALL - 988

## Suicide & Crisis Lifeline

We can all help prevent suicide. The 988 Lifeline provides 24/7, free and confidential support for people in distress, prevention and crisis resources for you or your loved ones, and best practices for professionals in the United States.

**DOMESTIC VIOLENCE HOTLINE**
**1-800-799-SAFE**
**WWW.THEHOTLINE.ORG**

When your Ego

AMAZON PAGE for other books by:
FREDD CARROLL

FACEBOOK
Author Fredd Carroll

INSTAGRAM
@AuthorFredd

EMAIL
VSZ_PUBLISHING@OUTLOOK.COM

APPLE PODCAST
A DUDE IN THE HENHOUSE
R-RATED LIFE HUMOR

Made in the USA
Middletown, DE
06 November 2023